Advance Praise for *Generation Why Not?*®

"Entering what Klein refers to as the 'Miracle Field' was never my issue. My issue was feeling bummed out when I had to leave the Miracle Field and go to the 'un-fun place' to handle my day-to-day. I know there was another way, I just hadn't found it until I read this book. *Generation Why Not?*® has gifted me an implementation strategy that keeps me energetic while I ground my creations and succeed in business. Ruth grounds the esoteric in a way that reaches both the Fortune 500 CEO and the artist. How cool is that?"

Lyndsay Hailey,
Co-writer of *Magic Mike Live*,
Alumni of iO and The Second City National
Touring Company, Actor/Director

"Ruth Klein is a true, heart-centered business leader, one who offers medicine for the soul based on her decades of experience as an entrepreneur. In her brilliant new book, *Generation Why Not?*®, Ruth advocates for a new, innovative, solutions-oriented, and most importantly, conscious approach to business. If you're looking for a riveting new read that will help you up-level your life and business, this is a book you'll definitely want to check it out!"

Robert Mack,
Author of *Happiness from the Inside Out*

"The brilliant Ruth Klein has done it again. In this book, *Generation Why Not?*®, she cracks the code of Quantum Synchronicity® that is used by high achievers and makes it accessible to anyone who chooses to learn and follow the simplified principles laid out in this book. If you are someone who's frustrated with your current outcomes despite your best efforts or someone who wants to up-level your game exponentially with grace, this is the book for you! Get ready to experience the lasting fulfillment of your heart's true desire."

Hang Boge, 5X undefeated Acrobat Champion, CEO of Stretch Your Potential, Founder of You've Got Love

"Thank you, Ruth Klein for creating the first consciously motivated road map to productivity, efficiency, financial success, and peace of mind. In *Generation Why Not?*® Ruth reveals her groundbreaking theory of Quantum Synchronicity® which combines the best of 'conscious thinking' with grounded, ethical, business efficacy. Using spiritual psychology, inspiring and motivating stories, and clearly defined action steps, Ruth provides readers a way out of the external noise of everyday life and into a life filled with magical moments, financial abundance, peacefulness and joy."

Elaine Hall, Award-winning Author, Speaker, Coach, Founder of The Miracle Project profiled in the two-time Emmy Award-winning HBO film *Autism: The Musical*

"*Generation Why Not?*® has had a very big impact on my life at a time when I needed it most. Ruth Klein is an exceptional human being and when you apply these principals…EXPECT THE UNEXPECTED!"

Tanya Memme, Emmy-nominated TV Host, A&E's *Sell This House*

"*Generation Why Not?*® is eye-opening and filled with ground-breaking insights to pursue what you want, no matter where you are in life. If you want to succeed in your business and accelerate your growth in alignment with your true desires, then, this is a must read."

Lauren G, 360Connect, Founder & CEO,
Former Facebook executive

"Ruth Klein's *Generation Why Not?*® is a definite must read. As with her previous books, you'll discover innovative, creative, and valuable insights, along with the tools to implement them. This inspiring book will help you gain an understanding about this powerful and growing generation, which is energized by inspiration, touched by creativity, and driven by a mindset that is in focus and on a mission. Ruth will guide you through all the necessary steps, be there on your journey, and help you achieve full success in all areas of your life."

Starla Marie, Recording Artist, Songwriter,
Producer, Actress

"I really enjoyed the concept and the execution of your new book, *Generation Why Not?*® You've done an exciting job of distilling the difficult task of how people can germinate and execute their contributions, no matter their age, to become at least givers and potentially world-wide entrepreneurs. Who knew that it could be brought into a stepwise procedure to become a giver of one's art and/or talent in business or anything else. I loved your systematic approach."

Joseph M. Pundyk,
Solar Power & Chemical Engineer

"Ruth Klein has taken one of the most profound concepts in personal development and distilled it into a simple, concrete form so that anyone can now 'plug into' Quantum Synchronicity® to create the life they desire. *Generation Why Not?*® is a book that dissolves the barriers in a person's mind as to why something cannot be accomplished. It produces the necessary confidence and clarity that empowers one to take inspired action and that critical first step on their adventure even though the Universal Laws remain hidden from sight. This book is also a godsend to those who fail to follow their dreams because of their fear of public ridicule, for when they are now asked the question why, the answer should be Why Not?"

Joe Swinger
Author, *Awaken the Magic Within*, and
CEO & Founder, The Silver Linings Network

"Ruth Klein's new book, *Generation Why Not?*®, delivers a powerful and practical message that comes as welcome news: It's a new day and the old rules and limitations don't apply anymore. We can be whatever we want to be no matter our age or circumstances. No excuses. It's time to dream big and then get started! *Generation Why Not?*® can show you how.

Jill Griffin
CEO of The Jill Griffin Group,
Bestselling Author of *Customer
Loyalty: How to Earn It,
How to Keep It*

GENERATION WHY NOT?®

7 Principles to a Purposeful Business and
Life, Driven by Attitude, Not Age

Ruth Klein

Post Hill
PRESS

A POST HILL PRESS BOOK
ISBN: 978-1-64293-416-8
ISBN (eBook): 978-1-64293-417-5

Generation Why Not?®:
7 Principles to a Purposeful Business and Life,
Driven by Attitude, Not Age
© 2020 by Ruth Klein
All Rights Reserved

Cover art by Michael Willis

Post Hill Press, LLC
New York • Nashville
posthillpress.com

Published in the United States of America

CONTENTS

INTRODUCTION

"I think 99 times and find nothing.
I stop thinking, swim in silence, and the truth comes to me."
Albert Einstein

Have you ever wondered why you find yourself successfully doing some things and then other things not so much? Or have you been around people who are always wishing they could be, or do something, different, but never go for it, no matter how talented they are?

I've always been a rather happy person, and I don't really know why. I've experienced a great deal of trauma in my life: 1) almost died at birth, 2) the sudden death of both of my parents, 3) had very bad facial acne from ages thirteen through twenty, with facial scars to prove it, 4) divorced after a thirty-four-year marriage, and 5) both parents lived through the Holocaust.

As I was growing up, I always felt different. I don't know if that was because I was living in two different cultures, an Eastern

European culture at home and the American culture once I stepped outside. I didn't feel inferior, just very different.

I was born into a beautiful immigrant family, rich with love, fear, trauma, and soul. My parents spoke broken English and didn't know much about American culture. I learned about children's books, such as Dr. Seuss, when I started reading to my own children. My friends couldn't believe I was reading these books for the first time.

Since both of my parents worked six and a half days a week, I knew that, if I wanted to have a birthday party, I would need to invite, create, and host my own—which I did every year until sixth grade. What a gift—I learned to plan and implement, and I received cool gifts that my parents would never have known to buy for me.

To get my parents' attention since they worked long days, I ended up becoming a great student, so I could make them proud. What a gift—my love of learning and reading has served me well. On the flip side, it also encouraged me to be a people pleaser.

When I really wanted to do something and my parents said, "No," I learned that it was a temporary "no" and, if I kept reminding them that I really wanted to do something or go somewhere, it usually turned into a tentative "yes." What a gift, as I learned to be persistent. Some family members would say stubborn.

My dad would ask me every year starting in second grade if I wanted to go to summer school, while giving me his gorgeous smile. To this day, I melt when a man shines a huge, sweet smile my way. I learned how to type in the fourth grade, and as a result of taking all the extra classes in high school summer school, I was able to graduate from high school a year early. What a gift—I learned to be productive and put time to good use. On the flip side, I also learned to "push" myself and became driven to succeed.

I grew up in a family where my parents lived through, miraculously, what the Power of One can do:

One word: Jew

One feeling: Hatred

One action: Genocide

During the Holocaust, my dad lived underground...literally...in a small hole with people stacked on top of one another. Bathroom facilities were nonexistent, and food was scarce. He showed me a place on his leg that had started to rot and was scarred over.

He lived, from the age of seventeen, a life of tremendous fear that the Nazis would find him or Polish neighbors would see him and let the Nazis know. And yet it was a non-Jewish Polish woman who saved my dad's life and the lives of three others. My dad was one in a family of twelve, and only he and a brother and sister survived.

My mom was one in a family of nine; at the tender age of twelve, she saw her parents and siblings die, and then she was sent to the concentration camp Auschwitz. She always wondered why she was the one who survived and, as a result, lived with survivor's guilt.

But I'm not here to share with you the atrocities that my parents witnessed and for which they had nightmares for most of their lives. Rather, I wanted to share three gifts I was blessed to learn because of my parents' traumatic experiences and how those experiences showed up in my life. Their experiences also taught me that the human Spirit is strong, and new Thoughts, Beliefs, and Behaviors are possible through the most severe types of trauma.

Gift #1: The Choice to live a life that is life-affirming versus life-destructive for me and others—and the Power of One.

One light breaks through darkness.

One word can build self-esteem. One feeling of love can heal broken hearts and spirits. One action can change the world, for better or for worse.

When things broke in my home, my parents would say in Yiddish, "This break over another break." Why? Because "stuff" to my parents was only stuff. Stuff wasn't valuable, but family, health, and education were very important.

Gift #2: The Courage to never, never give up…no matter how difficult the circumstances. I inherited my parents' consciousness of fear, but also of persistence. How did that show up in my life?

- My Achilles' heel has always been "security"—wanting to feel secure, safe, and protected.
- I learned to be fearful of planes until one day, shortly after my mom passed, I remember being on a plane and feeling calm for the first time. I felt that I was somehow closer to Mom, and from that day forward, I was no longer a white-knuckled and anxious plane traveler.
- I experienced a devastating divorce that brought on a huge amount of fear and anxiety, and left my life upturned and completely devastated.

And, after working on these fears and my need for security, I realized my security does not lie outside myself. My circumstances do not define me, just as my parents' security did not define them! Rather, the real gold lies within me—my creativity, my resourcefulness, my persistence, and my loving nature. This is my true security. And, when I finally came to that insight, I was able to move forward in peace and create a new and abundant life with lots of loving energy.

Gift #3: The Attitude of Possibility and always asking, "Why Not?" I opened up a women's dress shop when I was nine months pregnant. Nine months earlier, before I knew I was pregnant, I complained to my dad that there wasn't a professional women's clothing store in my small town and he said, "Why don't you open one?" And, of course, I thought, *Why Not?* and I did.

Another example of the attitude of possibility struck when my children had an elective two hours on Fridays and I didn't like the offerings the school gave, so I asked the principal if the school could start a theater class. She said, "No, but you can do it." What? And then I thought, *Why Not?* even though I had no idea how I was going to do that every Friday, which was a workday for me. Plus, I was a theater appreciator, but never the creator or director.

The class wrote a musical called *Greece*, using music from the *Grease* soundtrack. Since the school didn't have a stage, I suggested that we perform it on a professional stage. I was always a theater patron and, as crazy as it sounded at the time, I said, "Why Not?" and we made it happen. The students performed for a live audience, who loved them! How do I know this to be true?

Because the children received a standing ovation! And I received a bouquet of red, long-stemmed roses.

So, at the end of the day, I make a conscious choice to see through rose-colored lenses and live a life that is life-affirming and not take things personally, as it is only someone else's perception. I also found the internal courage of where my real security lies, able to turn challenges into seeing the blessings and the abundant gifts that show up, when I show up and stay open to possibility....

In the pages before you, I invite you to "remember" and see more clearly your true Self, your brilliance, talents, loving heart, internal courage, and the Power of One—You! You *get* to—not *have* to—choose the life you want and deserve!

Why Not?

Let's get started!

CHAPTER 1

THE NEW DEMOGRAPHIC SHIFT

*"Decide what you want.
Believe you can have it. Believe you deserve it
and believe it's possible."*
Jack Canfield

Traditional demographics have been falling out of favor for a few years in most industries, from law to entertainment. In fact, CBS—which is in partnership with Nielsen Media Research—no longer uses the old, tired, and unsuccessful demographic model of age, gender, and income to help businesses understand today's consumer. Indeed, the "Tiffany Network" calls the old method for determining TV viewership via the Nielsen ratings "hazardous to the marketer and business."

In addition, businesses are experiencing this new demographic shift within their workforce, from Millennials to Baby Boomers, in the form of employee conflict. I invite businesses, corporate executives, and business thought leaders to embrace this new perceptual demographic shift that will help them find and keep talent, the most competitive advantage that exists for a company to be successful, relevant, and sustainable in the twenty-first century.

This debate isn't a new one, as marketers and technology vendors have attempted in myriad ways to replace the old system, which looks primarily at factors such as age and gender to create audience segments. Now, as large companies begin to move away from demographics toward more in-depth insights based on "mental models" of the consumer (rather than labels such as "connected consumers" or "Baby Boomers"), technology and the digital agencies are ready for a paradigm shift.

In this book, I have expanded on the "mental model" to include the inter-correlation between the science of Quantum Physics and psychologist Carl Jung's work on Synchronicity and the unconscious. David Klein, CEO and co-founder of CommonBond, a financial technology company in New York that helps lower the cost of a college degree in the US, says that he focuses on three attributes when hiring talent at his company, which has about 100 employees today: Smart, Nice, and Hungry, no matter their age.

"We hire people regardless of what chronological generation they come from," Klein explains. "I'm looking for 'Smart,' meaning they have horsepower—a strong engine, judgment has to be good and they have to piece things together that might not make sense in a vacuum. They're able to put things together in a creative and practical way.

"'Nice' to mean that you're always respectful. It also means being direct with people and very honest and very candid—all in a way that is kind."

Klein goes on to say, "'Hungry' means they have an internal fire to perform at their highest level…internal motivation. They don't need external validation to get them going…they have an internal fire that keeps them focused and determined. It drives natural curiosity, which leads to finding the right answer and implementing it."

"On 'Curiosity,'" Klein says, "it's important for my people to question the status quo. To always be thinking or asking, 'What if we do it another way?' It's also about being genuinely open to what others have to say," adds Klein (who, in the interest of full disclosure, is my son).

In this book we will examine this new "mental model" paradigm through a new and disruptive perceptual lens that I call Quantum Synchronicity®. If you want entrepreneurial innovation, success, and sustainability in the new normal, this is how you do it. The old, tired, and true ways will only create friction in the workplace and lead to an unfulfilled team on every level.

And this is not industry specific. Businesses of all kinds can benefit from this new demographic shift and be prepared to embrace and engage in this perceptual shift that is being driven by attitude, mindset, personality, and other internal values, not age.

I introduce new proven Quantum Synchronicity® strategies to solve individual and employee conflicts between the different age groups in business. These same strategies work within families and communities. And, as David Klein shares, they all start with fueling up the "internal ignition." This new demographic shift is allowing women, men, and children to honor who they are and not allow their birthdates or external circumstances to stop them from reaching their dreams. Whether it's to write a book, start a new business, change careers, start a second or third career, or uplevel their businesses and lives two- to tenfold and beyond, at the end of the day, Why Not?

The people interviewed in this book, case studies, and personal experiences include all ages in business, sports, science, health, film, medicine, art, and technology. This new demographic shift will surprise you, inspire you, and propel you to become the best you can be now, no matter your age. Because this new shift knows that it's about your Intentions, Thoughts, Beliefs, Decisions, Actions, and Attitude.

All this has created an entirely new demographic, one that is much more predictive than the old one:

Generation Why Not?® uses its internal force or drive to activate leadership, innovation, creativity, and high performance.

Is It Age, or Is It an Internal Drive Using Talents and Looking Through a Different Perceptual Filter?

Age Twelve

• The youngest *New York Times* bestselling author finishes his first book—Jake Marcionette

Age Thirteen

- He writes his first software computer program—Bill Gates
- She begins writing her famous diary just before she goes into forced hiding from the Nazis—Anne Frank

Age Fifteen

- She wins the gold medal in women's figure skating at the Olympic Winter Games in Nagano, Japan—Tara Lipinski

Age Twenty-one

- He introduces a new computer, created with a colleague—Steve Jobs
- He wins his first Masters in golf and becomes the youngest winner—Tiger Woods

Age Twenty-nine

- He invents the telephone—Alexander Graham Bell

Age Thirty-one

- He becomes a billionaire and at the time, he was the youngest person ever to reach that milestone—Bill Gates

- She discovers two elements, polonium and radium, founding a new scientific field—radioactivity —Marie Curie

Age Thirty-four

- After witnessing the bombardment of Fort McHenry, he wrote "The Star-Spangled Banner"—Francis Scott Key

Age Thirty-eight

- He develops a vaccine for the deadly virus polio— Dr. Jonas Salk

Age Forty-two

- He is awarded the 1921 Nobel Prize in Physics despite being a late bloomer to speak as a child—Albert Einstein

Age Fifty-one

- She becomes the first woman justice to serve on the US Supreme Court—Sandra Day O'Connor

Age Fifty-two

- She takes an art class with a friend for fun and a few years later is being commissioned to do art for clients— Beverley Barber

Age Fifty-six

- He completes the design for the Paris tower that will bear his name—Gustave Eiffel

Age Sixty-two

- He publishes the first volume of many for his fantasy series, *Lord of the Rings*—J.R.R. Tolkien

Age Seventy-one

- She develops a new and sustainable iconic fashion look, the Chanel suit—Coco Chanel

Age Seventy-seven

- He writes and publishes his first of four books—Arsen Marsoobian

Age Eighty-three

- The baby doctor becomes an activist for world peace—Dr. Benjamin Spock

It becomes apparent then that age and gender, the old demographic lenses we used to look through, are no longer clear or helpful measurements to be used by businesses and consumers, managers and staff, founders, innovators, and creatives. It is clear that something else is going on in business and personal development.

If we "see" the workforce and ourselves through the lens of age—i.e., Millennials—and Boomers expect this group of workers to be selfish, ego driven, and obsessive, then that is likely what we'll receive while they're working with us.

People of all ages tend to rise to the expectation we place upon them. So, rather than separating each other in the workforce, what if we disrupted those old perceptual filters and saw people as people, rather than categorize them as too young, too old, or too anything? At the end of the day, *why not* try it and see what happens within your own organization, family, community?

This is how Generation Why Not?® sees the world. They see things as they could be, not as they are at this moment. As Wayne Gretzky, the famous hockey player, said, *"A good hockey player plays where the puck is. A great hockey player plays where the puck is going to be."* And business, just as in sports, requires this new way of thinking. It gives them the momentum and curiosity and, from there, it is easier to create, innovate, and make a bigger impact to find solutions to problems. Problems solved in the quantum arena of possibility are much more powerful and effective than in the muck of the problem! Keep your eyes on the moving target.

The New Demographics is based more on the mental, behavioral, and emotional processes of these groups. Getting more in depth and personal, realizing the vastness of attitudes and beliefs of these generations, made perfect sense when I read a recent *Los Angeles Times* front page article headlined, "Tech titans fuel a scramble to build large-scale offices.... Landlords are ripping out escalators, walls in pursuit of new kind of tenant."

So many of the tech giants are turning into media moguls. They are turning closed-in malls and other large spaces into airy urban campuses for these content creators because of the New Demographic Shift.

I remember visiting one of my friend's son's offices at a Fortune 500 company. I was horrified...literally horrified that he was working in such stifled quarters that consisted of a small cubicle with no personal space except his boring desk and chair, little privacy, sharp lights flooding the area, and stagnant energy throughout the building, without any open windows and air flow...and I'm a Baby Boomer! It reminded me of an assembly line with harsh lighting, torpid airflow, and no personalization...at all! What I saw was truly alarming. Everyone was really nice, but with its harsh fluorescent lighting and no personal space, the environment truly looked and felt like an assembly line for brilliant employees.

Generation Why Not?® is a new socio-statistical population entity that can include all ages. Why? Because the Generation Why Not?® framework of people's buying habits and interpersonal communications is based more on their internal traits or their Intentions, Thoughts, Beliefs, and Actions regarding what they want and what they're doing. They are aware of making their words intentional as they know words matter...both to themselves and with others. Their old beliefs that no longer serve them have been tested, and new, updated beliefs have been adopted; they commit and make decisions; they take inspired action; they take the momentum they create and sustain it; they have an awareness of their environments—from their emotional to their physical environment.

Baby Boomers—The Baby Boomers today are changing careers, doing the things they've always wanted to do and starting second and third acts, and they have the health and the time to do them, unlike the generation of Traditionalists before them. However, the Generation X-ers are also changing careers.

Generation X-ers—A little caught in the middle between Baby Boomers (their parents) and Millennials (the workforce underneath them), Generation X has a bit of an identity challenge going on.

Millennials—The dichotomy of the Millennials is between those who are unicorns and have the attitude to go with it, and those who are very smart and have an entitled attitude, or so we've heard.

Let's look at some new demographics for the different ages, although keep in mind that I'm doing this for easy understanding. Let's look at the similar Core Values across the three generational old demographic groups we've used in the past.

Baby Boomers—(Approximately between 1946–1964)

Generation X—(Approximately between 1965–1980)

Millennials—(Approximately between 1981–1996)

Looking at the similarities among all three—Baby Boomers, Gen X, and Millennials—you find...

- They all are suspicious of authority;
- They are highly educated;
- They have high job expectations.

As you look at the Core Values of Baby Boomers and Millennials, you see they are more similar than they are different.

- The environment is very important to them…the Baby Boomers started the hippie movement with their green thumbprint and environmental advocacy.
- Baby Boomers started sharing a lot of enlightenment and spirituality in their youth…similar to what Millennials are doing now.
- Both want to have a big impact to make this a better community and world. The Boomers started the healthy food and juice craze, as well as natural and healthy skin and food products.
- They are extremely loyal to their children.
- Personal gratification is important to both.

Generation Why Not?® embraces and engages with leaders and high performers by looking at how each older demographic model shares similarities. It is the similarities of these demographic generations that are going to create company harmony and, as a result, far less employee and management turnover, and higher productivity and profits. And, as an extension, the similarities will create internal harmony within businesses, families, and communities. We have the opportunity for a new way to communicate between these different age groups, focusing on similarities, as well as positive reinforcement and transparency, which are all key leadership core values and qualities!

In the next chapter, I will share with you how Generation Why Not?® is the generation that is going to be—and already is, and has been for decades—the leaders that are the innovators, the creative problem solvers, and the Generation that will move business and humanity forward, focused on what we *can* do, build, create, and innovate together, no matter your income, race, or birthdate!

Questions to ponder:

1. What is your present age?
2. What do you feel is your greatest strength?
3. Would you consider yourself a member of Generation Why Not?®

CHAPTER 2

WHAT *IS* GENERATION WHY NOT?®

"We must be willing to let go of the life we
planned so as to have the life that is waiting for us."
Joseph Campbell

I n this chapter, I'll be sharing with you the internal strategies that Generation Why Not?® entrepreneurs, multimillion-dollar start-ups, executives, "mompreneurs," creatives, and professional athletes share in common. You will find that this is a generation driven by attitude, not age.

The understanding of this powerful and growing generation is energized by inspiration…touched by creativity and driven by a mindset that is on focus and a mission. And why it is imperative that we embrace Generation Why Not?®

We are in an era of innovation and inclusion that will drive our economy to new heights of invention and solve some of the biggest problems in business and in social change worldwide.

And this Generation is set up for the challenge with their internal code, Quantum Synchronicity® (Chapter 3 is where I share this Generation's Internal Code).

I found there to be a thread, a commonality of what propels successful and "high-achieving" CEOs, founders of multimillion-dollar companies, high-earning entrepreneurs, and professional athletes and actors.

It's time to identify this generation and call it what it is. Members of Generation Why Not?® have been around throughout the ages and most likely were (and are) seen as disruptors. Yes, they are disruptors, in the best sense of the word. As the transcendental philosopher Henry David Thoreau would put it, Generation Why Not?® "marches to a different drumbeat" than most others do. Their ideas, at first glance, are thought of as impossible, or they're seen as dreamers that need to get a shot of reality. This Generation may hear other people's disbelief, but they continue to listen to their own strong heart and vision. Because, at the end of the day, they know they can do it!

They're not to be admired as much as they are to be seen as inspirational because they allow us to see what is possible. They empower each one of us to reinforce the sense that we can be a part of a vital and vivacious generation.

In fact, your heart's desire demands that of you!

Generation Why Not?® is a group that looks at education, inspiration, and implementation in a new way. It's a perceptual disruption in how we see ourselves, our failures, our outcomes, our businesses, and our lives, as well as the lens from which we see and act in the world.

Generation Why Not?® knows there needs to be a different perception in order to thrive in business and in their personal lives. This includes corporate cultures between different demographic generations; inspiration by showing what other "Generation Why Notters" are internally doing with their Intention, Thoughts, Beliefs, Decisions, Actions, Momentum, and Environment, which I refer to as the "7 Principles of Quantum Synchronicity®" (I go into detail on this in the next chapter).

Why the Need for Generation Why Not?® Exists *Now*

I saw a need, a big need, both in terms of American workers' growth and productivity, plus the personal needs and desires of men and women who make up the workforce, no matter what their age or industry is.

I spoke with several of my colleagues in businesses losing hundreds of thousands to millions of dollars because of a demotivated workforce, largely due to the communication clashes Millennials and Baby Boomers experienced at work, as many belonging to Generation Y (Millennials) were managing workers seven to twenty years older than they were.

According to research by the University of Scranton, 92 percent of people do not achieve their goals. That translates into individuals who are frustrated, overwhelmed, and demotivated as a result of being unfulfilled, including not attaining their dream business, career, or authentic lifestyle.

Research has found that lack of motivation and happiness on the job costs the US between $550 and $750 billion in lost productivity each year.

Members of Generation Why Not?® still have anxiety and issues related to being in business, although they are much less severe and far less often, as they know how to change direction when that happens. They don't wallow long in negativity.

This Generation is upending the established way of seeing and doing things and conventional wisdom by making waves with new ways of thinking and acting. Ralph Waldo Emerson said, "Do not go where the path may lead, go instead where there is no path and leave a trail." In so many ways, this is analogous to creating new neural pathways in the brain by thinking new thoughts and taking new actions.

My experience consulting; developing strategic plans; and coaching entrepreneurs, high-performance leaders, thought leaders, and transformational coaches reinforced the notion that many of them were sabotaging much of their own innovative ideas in business and financial success due to obsessive thinking or self-doubt, anxiety, procrastination, and emotional turmoil. These negative attributes became self-fulfilling prophecies, roadblocks to their own success!

According to psychologists and health care professionals, there is a huge increase in people feeling anxious about their lives, mostly created by their limiting thoughts and beliefs. Interviewing high-performance entrepreneurs and executives, I have found in my research that limiting beliefs can stifle success in ways you couldn't even imagine. The difficult part of this is that most people do not see their "blind spots." It is these "off-screen areas" that continue to take us off course. Later in this book, I'll share how many entrepreneurs and executives were able to change course once they became aware of self-defeating thoughts and beliefs that were severely holding them back from attaining the success they knew they could reach, in their businesses and personal lives.

Second and Third Acts

Generation Why Not?® includes Second and Third Acts. These acts two and three play vital roles in this new generation…from people in corporate jobs to becoming entrepreneurs, sculptors, or writers…from fifty-somethings to octogenarians re-creating themselves in order to fulfill their entrepreneurial dreams, or people who want to have "Do Overs" from their twenties to eighties. A friend of mine in her late twenties went into law because her father was a lawyer, but two years into it, she could only think of getting out of it. She went back to school to study psychology and became a business coach with a strong legal background. She told me, "I want to do this over again and go into the field that inspires me, not wipes me out."

This generation is innovative, purposeful, passionate, alive, creative, and resourceful. Those who are part of Generation Why Not?® are Perceptual Disruptors of what can be accomplished in business and in their lives. They see situations and circumstances differently than others do, and while they may be afraid, they move past their fears and do it anyway. My friend who changed careers felt fear on two fronts: the money she spent on law school, including taking out loans, and her parents' reaction. However, what she wanted outweighed the fear of staying "miserable," as she says. Your dream has to be stronger than your fear.

They know there is more to their businesses and lives and are willing to go beyond the fear to reach their dreams. They are innovators...they constantly look for new ways to solve problems.

The Fifteen Factors That Make Up Generation Why Not?®

This Generation is intentional with their success.

They know words matter.

They are conscious of their thinking and redirect their thoughts to stay grounded and purpose driven.

They take action, regardless of their moods.

They protect their environment, internally as well as externally.

They are inspired to act when others say something can't be done.

They know there's a lot to be done and they are the ones to do it.

They rarely take "no" for an answer.

They are resourceful and keep trying new things in new ways.

They feel the fear and don't let that stop them.

They capitalize on their natural strengths, brilliance, talents, and skills.

They know the importance of mentors and coaches.

They are innovators...they constantly look for new ways to solve problems.

They often ask how things can be better, smoother, simpler... often asking themselves, "Why Not?" in terms of doing something differently, engaging differently, thinking differently, and believing differently.

They make things happen…even though they don't know how to do it or where to start…they know the power in just starting!

This generation, more than any other, feels in alignment with their purpose in their work, dreams, or volunteering.

Generation Why Not?® Knows Words Matter!

I was looking through my Instagram and saw a post by a friend and colleague, Michelle Perkins, a Certified Money Coach, and she looked up the word "work" in the dictionary. Here's a sampling of the synonyms for work: *drudge, exertion, grind, muscle, obligation, pains, push, servitude, slogging, stint, stress, striving, effort, industry, job, performance, struggle, task, trial, attempt.* OK, you get the idea. Is it any wonder that we see work as tough, hard drudgery?

Here are some synonyms for the word "work" from the perceptual lens of Generation Why Not?® This Generation knows words matter!

Synonyms: *Gratitude, inspired action, purpose driven, social responsibility, consciousness, present, meaningful, reimagined, miracle, energy field, manifestation, energy, Quantum Synchronicity®, learning, insights, Divinely Gifted Downloads, resourcefulness, creative, innovative, feedback, life-serving, commitment, personal responsibility,* and *action,* to name a few.

Who Can Benefit from This Perceptual Shift in Business?

Entrepreneurs—Generation Why Not?® is for entrepreneurs who feel stuck, overwhelmed, stressed out, and frustrated that their businesses are not working; find they are tired of what they're doing in their businesses; have always had a dream to do something different but were afraid to try to do it because of their age or their circumstances. Professional actors, professional athletes, and realtors, to name a few, go under this heading as well because, in the "truest" sense, they are entrepreneurs of their career and talent, and those who realize this early on are the most successful and financially stable. All people in the "creative arts" are entrepreneurs, and those who are Generation Why Not?® find great personal and financial success as a result.

Corporate C-level executives and managers—Those in corporate America who are having a greater challenge integrating the personalities and motivations within their workforce—primarily, the Millennials, Generation X, and Baby Boomers. This challenge is showing up in their bottom line and productivity rate, as well as causing high turnover of talent.

This new internal values code of this Generation will help C-level executives and managers understand the motivation and commonalities behind Generation Why Not?® so that they can utilize this information to retain talent, allow for innovation and creativity, and increase employee motivation and their bottom line through a more harmonious employee culture across several generational demographics.

Business Thought Leaders—Those who look for ways to help their companies and boards find and keep talent in their business and those of their clients' businesses. They seek new ideas and creative strategies to continue business profits and productivity moving forward in this highly competitive talent pool of innovations.

Mompreneurs—Finally, a place where women entrepreneurs feel understood and are encouraged to go out on their own, if that is what they want…to start or scale a business at any age. The only things that matter are their attitude, mindset, and desire. They find in Generation Why Not?® the acceptance, without apologizing for or defending what or why they're stepping out to be an entrepreneur. It doesn't matter if they were a high-powered attorney or a top-level executive in corporate America before they became mothers. No longer do they feel guilty for going after what they want, and there's a whole generation that supports, encourages, and empowers them to be the best they can be!

Twenty-somethings—Generation Why Not?® is finally a tribe that understands these young adults who want to pursue their dreams on their own terms rather than be governed or pressured into doing what their parents or others think they should be or do. They want to know that they can dream; be passionate about their vision; be supported; work with focus, commitment, and consistency; and create a successful business and life.

This book, *Generation Why Not?®*, gives all these groups and others a valuable stream of information to help facilitate their expertise, using a new and disruptive perceptual business model based on Quantum Synchronicity® (the next chapter goes into Quantum Synchronicity® in detail).

How Generation Why Not?®
Integrates Their Brand Print into Their
Conscious Leadership DNA

Our Brand Print is the essence of who we are. Every person has a different fingerprint, even identical twins. The same goes for business brands. Once you understand the essence of your brand, your marketing messaging will flow more easily and the authenticity of who you are as an entrepreneur or the corporate culture from which you work. Then it will be easier to enroll new clients and charge a premium for your services with a high perceptual value.

You create a strong Brand Print with a brand and not a product. Just think of which one has a more positive effect on you… an Apple computer or just a "computer"?

Generation Why Not?® is part of a corporate or an entrepreneur's business brand. Everyone has a unique Brand Print. It is this Brand Print that you must identify, understand, and share with your ideal clients. This Brand Print says exactly who you are and how you're different.

I also like to say that the process of identifying your Conscious Leadership DNA is also the essence of who you are as a person, as an entrepreneur, and as a world citizen, and it is the lens from which you see and interact in the world—the impact you want to make and not only with your message but with the passion or the "why" behind it.

Conscious Leadership DNA

Your leadership DNA is the essence of who you are at the core. And, if you're not clear on your values and how your business reflects these values, you're missing out on a lot of dollars, ideal clients, creative talent, and market message clarity.

This Generation's leadership platform is based on several of the following heartfelt beliefs:

- People are basically good.
- You can always find something to compliment in a person.
- Businesses should share by spreading their good fortune as the gifts of social responsibility.
- Limiting beliefs can be transformed with awareness, compassion, support, and learning new ways.
- Vulnerability is brave and courageous.
- Life is to be fully lived.
- Ideas are only as good as their implementation.
- Trust is a core value to success.
- The Universal Laws are real and unbending.
- Listening through heart-centered "eyes" improves communication.
- A positive attitude is a person's most attractive feature.

- Strive to show up authentically and honestly.
- Environment is more powerful than genetics.
- Creating a purpose-rich and financially profitable business is important.
- Every day is an opportunity to share love and kindness.
- Persistence and focus are core values.
- Loving words are magical notes to the Spirit.
- Our greatest blessings come from our most challenging teachers.
- Quantum Synchronicity® is real.

Questions to ponder:

1. Which of the Conscious Leadership qualities are important to you?
2. Which of the Conscious Leadership qualities, if implemented, would make a positive impact on you, your business, and your life?

CHAPTER 3

QUANTUM SYNCHRONICITY®

> *"Two roads diverged in a wood, and I—*
> *I took the one less traveled by,*
> *And that has made all the difference."*
> Robert Frost

Quantum Synchronicity® integrates Quantum Physics and Carl Jung's Synchronicity, as well as my own methodology, to produce Quantum Synchronicity®: The Method. The Method consists of Seven Principles and is the framework for how this new Generation thinks, believes, and acts. For over two decades, I have used these seven principles with entrepreneurs and CEOs to help them achieve innovative and successful businesses and lives. The term Quantum Synchronicity® refers to Quantum Theory (energetic patterns in the physical world) and Carl Jung's definition of Synchronicity (meaningful coincidence of two or more factors). The science of personal energy, the mechanics of consciousness, and our attitude are the three most important natural factors affecting the outcomes of our goals and success, both in business and in life.

I call this connection between the strong energy charges and meaningful coincidences our Spirit DNA, which helps to direct our success. This Spirit DNA will make more sense for you when we look at real case examples.

Powerful Implications of Quantum Synchronicity® and Generation Why Not?®

So many people today feel as though they are on an unending treadmill, between changing priorities, long commutes, instant communication, and the need to immediately respond, an addictive attachment to technology and social media. The list goes on…. So how are we to live in our world, stay centered while we build a successful company or career, raise our families, help our children and parents if we are living in the sandwich years, have personal time, have fun, and take time off now and again? The list goes on….

The answer—as I found in my own life, through my research and working with clients in all industries, socioeconomic levels, and ages—lies in the integration of using the Seven Principles of Quantum Synchronicity® every day, in one way or another. And those who do, regardless of their age, find they're living in a quantum world of possibility and flow. The people who are conscious and aware of their thoughts, beliefs, and actions, and make conscious choices fall in the arena of Generation Why Not?®.

This Generation is driven by attitude, not age, and they have learned how to create habits that serve them; think thoughts that give them energy rather than drain them; believe they can live the life they desire without having to sacrifice their health, families, or natural resources; make choices that reinforce their desire to take an active approach to decision-making; take actions that reinforce their Intentions, Thoughts, and Beliefs; continue to build momentum as they take action; and guard their internal and external environments, including relationships to reflect what they do want...not what they don't want.

We are all human, and Quantum Synchronicity® is a framework for unlimited possibilities of creativity in building a business and life reimagined! Some people believe that their circumstances define them or that, because of their circumstances, they can't create the business or life they desire. Both of these thoughts work on a consciousness of limitation. They start to show up as roadblocks along your desired path that seem too big to overcome. The longer you hold on to these limiting thoughts and beliefs, the longer your business lingers outside what you truly want. Later, I'll share stories with you of an autistic teen, Coby Bird, who works as an actor and takes risks every day to be the best he can be; and Neal Katz, an autistic young adult, who gives paid speeches and is nationally recognized, even though he can't speak. They and many others in this Generation did not allow their circumstances or fear to define them.

What Quantum Synchronicity®: The Method will show is how these Seven Principles have influenced the men and women who make up Generation Why Not?® and how they can and did alter the course of their businesses and lives by opening up to the possibility of a new paradigm shift. And Quantum Synchronicity® is the framework for this paradigm shift that Generation Why Not?® uses…an integration of the science of personal energy, the mechanics of consciousness and meaningful coincidences woven into everyday occurring events. It is this integration that impacts our businesses, families, finances, health, communities, relationships…basically everything we do.

Quantum Synchronicity®: The Method

The Seven Principles of Quantum Synchronicity® are (in order):

1. **Intention**—Intention leads the direction…the idea… the dream and directs consciousness creation. Intention is the direction that we want our businesses and lives to take. Oprah Winfrey interviewed Gary Zukav on one of her *SuperSoul Sunday* programs and said that, after reading Zukav's book, *The Seat of the Soul,* and learning about Intention, she used a specific Intention to bring about spiritual topics and conversation on more enlightened subjects. Oprah believes that this Intention is what helped her TV show be in the top daytime ratings for twenty-five years.

2. **Thought**—All thoughts are energy, and all successful manifestation first starts with thought…and the words to support our thoughts and what we desire. Thoughts are transferred to your words. Your thoughts are "invisi-

ble" energy and give momentum to what you think about, whether positive or negative. Our feelings come from our thoughts and underlying beliefs. Thoughts themselves are neutral. It is the positive or negative meaning we give to thoughts that create our life, literally. Change your thoughts and you can change your life.

3. **Belief**—Beliefs inform you and your values and are the powerful precursors to seeing your success…or seeing your limitations. Generation Why Not?® sees themselves as they want to be as they move toward their goals, desires, and dreams…not from where they are presently. It's very similar to what Wayne Gretzky, the Stanley Cup award-winning ice hockey player, said about his success, "I skate to where the puck is going to be, not where it has been." If you believe that Quantum Physics and consciousness play a vital role in your energy and that everything is energy, you start to see a direct cause and effect between your beliefs and how the transformation of these beliefs to transcend what you "see" right now in your life are the result of your thoughts and beliefs yesterday. They can be changed in seconds to reflect a new, more updated belief system that offers you the future you desire. And, as opposed to conventional wisdom, changing your thoughts and beliefs does not have to take a long time.

4. **Decision**—Decisions are pivotal moments impacted by pivotal situations or events we've experienced. Your deci-

sions either empower you or disempower you, and how you make decisions gives clarity on the choices available to you. Decisions allow you to take action through your commitments to yourself and also to others. It's living life from a perspective of taking the leap into the unknown and allowing the Universe to take it from there. The truth is, we are living in the "unknown" every second of every day. Just ask anyone who lived through 9/11. Thinking we have complete control over our lives is one of the biggest fallacies in our thinking. We can, however, control our Intentions, Thoughts, Beliefs, Decisions, and Actions.

5. **Action**—Action is the sum of our Intentions, Thoughts, Beliefs, and Decisions. All the Intention and good thoughts in the world do not work without taking action—and taking action, in spite of feeling over-whelmed, fearful, or stuck. When you find yourself put-ting things off and not taking action, the best place to look for clarity of the resistance and new insights is in your Intentions, Thoughts, or Beliefs. Most likely, you have what is referred to as Paradoxical, or competing, Intentions, Thoughts, or Beliefs active in your subcon-scious. And, since it's the subconscious that is in the driver's seat, it is here—the place of "default" you go to—if you're not present and conscious at the moment.

6. **Momentum**—Momentum is the energy, the certainty, and the movement that happens when you take the

slightest action. You must have motion for momentum to occur. And, once you're in momentum, you want to "guard" and "protect" this energy without interruptions.

7. **Environment**—Environment is an all-encompassing internal and external spectrum that includes thoughts, emotions, physical space, the body, spirit, friends, colleagues, even how you "hold" money and time! How you embrace and engage in your different environments either supports you or drains you.

I heard a quote from a friend and don't know if she created it or if she read it, but I loved it so much I wrote it down: "If you had to fit in, you wouldn't have stood out." Generation Why Not?® feels "different" or "unique," and they're good with it. They know they do not want to fit in to the everyday unconscious or the default habit of just going through the motions of their life, without really experiencing fully the special moments. If life is made up of special moments, don't you want to be part of that adventure?

It is in this Quantum Synchronicity® "soup" where everything happens…new ideas, creativity, innovation, and transformation! I like to say that Quantum Synchronicity® is the integration of your Brand Print and your Spirit. It helps you look within to make a powerful impact outwardly and, as a result, you put into motion creativity, personal resourcefulness, and powerful authenticity integrated with your talents, passions, and dreams.

I share with my clients that, once they become aware of Quantum Synchronicity® in their lives, they will find it all around them and begin to anticipate its real effects in and on their lives, as well as the impact they're making on others. You will start to "see" how the unknown converts into the known through the Seven Principles of manifesting your desires…or not.

And all your manifestation is simply feedback. And it's this feedback that, if you don't like it, you can go to the framework of the Seven Principles and see where you could think different thoughts, create new beliefs around what is true for you today, make different choices and take different action.

In addition, you'll start to see how so many ideas and people start coming together to produce a reality of possibility much greater than its parts. A "predictable X factor" begins to emerge. Quantum Synchronicity® brings together the seen and unseen forces. You start to *believe* it before you can *see* it, because you have a strong sense knowing that, just because you can't see it right now, it doesn't mean it's not here…or coming.

In my Branding & Communications Strategic Consulting and Coaching, the clients I have worked with using Quantum Synchronicity®: The Method range from small entrepreneurs to Fortune 500 companies. Here are a few of the results I've been blessed to be a part of:

- A Millennial CEO of a start-up company worked with me on his business and personal branding and watched how these principles helped him create a $300 million-plus company within six years.
- A corporate executive who became an entrepreneur without any clients attained a full client load, earning over $250,000 within nine months of our working together.

- An excellent and introverted attorney brought in a $1 million-plus new client to the firm, with my guidance.
- A large supplement company needed my help creating its new branded products…from naming the products to writing the brand messaging to getting them into GNC for consumers to purchase within six months.
- A solopreneur asked me to help her rewrite an existing book that wasn't selling, turning it into a new book that attracted new clients. She had her first $10,000 week within months of the newly published book.
- A financial consultant and stockbroker needed more ideal clients for her son, who was starting in the firm. Within twelve weeks of contracting with me, both she and her son were so busy she couldn't return my calls.
- A very talented singer/songwriter brought in $100,000 within two weeks of working with me, 2.5 times more money than she had ever made in one year.
- A new coach needed help attracting her ideal clients, so we created her programs and signature speech, after which she started earning the most she had ever made financially with a purpose-driven business. Most recently, she was asked to give a TEDx Talk after the director heard the speech we worked on together.
- A talented new children's author and illustrator started a business for the first time in her life after volunteering her gifts for the last eighteen years and had an article written about her and her new enterprise within a few months of starting her business.

- An entrepreneur left the corporate world to start her own business three years ago, and, within the first six weeks of my working with her, she attracted twice as much money in twelve months as she had in the previous three years combined.
- An Emmy award-winning entrepreneur and coach tripled her income within eighteen months of our working together and now charges three times what she first charged years earlier, with happy clients and excellent results!

How is it possible that so many people listed above and with whom I've worked have had similar results?

The answer to that question is the heart and soul of this book, *Generation Why Not?*® and uses the framework of the Seven Principles of Quantum Synchronicity®. Quantum Synchronicity® is a proven method showing how you are at the center of a world with unlimited potential, power, and possibilities activated by the invisible energy force of the Universe!

Quantum Synchronicity® is a method to help further explain what is actually happening in the lives of members of Generation Why Not?® who reach out and make an impact in their businesses, lives, families, finances, health, communities, and relationships, with science to back it up.

Quantum Physics and Consciousness have opened up a whole new world where we have more control over our lives and future than we thought possible. If you can open up to this perceptual shift of unlimited possibilities, then you are stepping into this Generation. This new paradigm shift allows you to be incredibly creative, more communicative with others, and profoundly innovative, while owning your personal authentic power by being conscious of your Intentions, Thoughts, Beliefs, Decisions, Actions, Momentum, and Environment.

The Dynamics of Quantum Physics

Quantum Physics reveals the uncertainty theory that says there are unending possibilities as to what we have the power to create. And it further says that the world is in a constant state of change whereby even the smallest shift in energy can create an immediate and far-reaching transformation in your reality. And, while the majority of the power in the Universe can't be seen, it nonetheless exists to great effect. And your personal vibration is nonetheless affected by this unseen power!

A lot of new science was found when researchers of Quantum Physics discovered that everything—seen and unseen—is vibrating strings of energy. Those things that we previously thought to be solid matter, like a piece of furniture, for example, are really composed of energy vibrations. And, to make it even more exciting, it was scientifically found that consciousness has influence over these vibrations.

And, just when it couldn't get more fascinating, researchers went further to scientifically reveal that it is this interconnectedness of consciousness and energy that determines all the outcomes we experience in all aspects of our life: business, health, finances, romances. In fact, you are creating your future right now...with your consciousness (thoughts) and energy.

And, if this is the first or twentieth time you've heard or read this, I'm going to walk you through this process in layman's terms that you can understand and show you real-life examples of people living Generation Why Not?® lives to further demonstrate to you the unending possibilities of empowering yourself to change and live the life you desire.

I was incredibly curious about Quantum Physics from the moment I learned about it. Finally, it made perfect sense to me.

I remember working on a project for my Master's in Spiritual Psychology and I was walking very early in the morning...the moon was still out, and I remember it was a full bright moon and I was captivated by it.

I told my walking partner to look at that gorgeous moon and, when I looked up to show him, it was out of sight! How could that be...it was just seconds from the moment I gazed at it and then looked back at it again.

It was at that moment that it became very clear to me that "just because I can't see it, it doesn't mean it's not there."

And then a light bulb came on in full force. Just because I can't "see" electricity doesn't mean it's not there. And because I can't "see" gravity doesn't mean it doesn't exist.

And then, as I learned more about Quantum Physics, I realized that the natural world consists of energy and consciousness. And that everything is energy...a vibration. And part of Quantum Physics is the uncertainty theory that says we live in a world of possibilities and we have a hand in opening up those possibilities for ourselves.

The natural order of things, according to Quantum Physics, is an order that is in constant flux. And a very small change in energy in one area, no matter how small, affects change else-where. Quantum physics has no regard for linear time. One small energy shift has a huge impact in Quantum Physics as it has on our daily lives.

This shift happens at the smallest level (quantum), including on a cellular level within our bodies. And what has seemed like a mystery up until now is based on scientific patterns. Consciousness, frequency, and energy are in constant motion, vibrating within and around you in a celebration of the "magic" within you and within the Universe. It is this source of energy that directs your destiny, and when you decide to live here, you'll find that your business and life have been blessed beyond what you could have even imagined!

This invisible force of the Universe is no longer mystical or mythical. You're vibrating energy right now, as is all of the Universe. This is the moment…right here, right now, where you can take dominion—mastery over your life and align with the field of possibilities!

This alignment works whether you're applying it to your small business, corporate culture, or personal relationships.

In short, according to German physicist David Bohm, the reader will start to see their world as fundamentally connected, not made up of fragments or made up of separate situations. Einstein once quoted David Bohm as saying, "There is a sense of destiny that travels with us all the time, if we choose to take the time and 'see' it." This is the underlining idea behind the energy and meaningful coincidences of Generation Why Not?®.

The Laws of the Universe are real, stable, and don't bend. In some ways, it's like my computer. If I hit one incorrect letter or number, I simply won't reach the web address I'm looking for…or connect via email to the right person. And I can only do certain tasks in Word—if I try to bend the rules, even a bit, it doesn't work.

And, if you understand how Quantum Synchronicity® shows up in your life, you can have more control over the way you want to create your business and your life! One of the reasons that we stay "stuck" or work in a business we don't like is because we have created patterns that don't serve us. And, just as we created the patterns and habits that don't serve us, we can just as easily create new ones.

When we start applying the Laws of the Universe, Quantum Physics, and Synchronicity, we set in motion a new world of creativity and possibility. Some people would refer to this as magic. I don't see it as magic, but I definitely do feel it's magical!

Generation Why Not?® through the principles of Quantum Synchronicity®, tap into this invisible field of energy to uncover unlimited power, creativity, and pure potential to create success, value, and purpose in businesses and lives. In order to experience this new frontier, you need to open up to a new perceptual lens from which to see and interact with yourself and the Universe.

In This Book

This book is written to first introduce you to a new demographic and the members of this growing group, Generation Why Not?®, as well as the Seven Principles of Quantum Synchronicity® and how these ideas and principles can be used to live a life of purpose, meaning, and passion in business and in life.

I've designed this book to offer you support as well as the possibility of opening up to heart-centered experiential learning. I invite you to keep a journal, so you can record any epiphanies that you might have.

Each of the seven chapters on the principles of Quantum Synchronicity® includes:

- Bonus Breakthrough training online to go deeper into each process and principles
- Stories and examples to help you further your understanding
- A meditation to prepare your mind, body, and spirit to digest and help connect with your subconscious to open up to what is possible for you
- A suggested song to celebrate the essence of each of the Seven Principles

It is with deep gratitude that I have enjoyed experiencing Quantum Synchronicity® as a member of Generation Why Not?® while also supporting clients in doing the same.

It is my hope that this book, the exercises, and bonus downloads will help empower you to take inspired action to live a purpose-driven and financially profitable business and life.

My intention is that you remember how special and unique you are as well as your Divinely gifted talents. I hope you feel the inspiration and support every step of the way. May your journey be mostly lived in the Invisible Miracle Field where dreams come true, relationships are reimagined, and you have the opportunity to "see" the world and your experiences as blessings!

Questions to ponder:

1. Which of the Seven Principles of Quantum Synchronicity® would you like to flex more muscle?
    -   Intention
    -   Thought
    -   Belief
    -   Decision
    -   Action
    -   Momentum
    -   Environment

Bonus Download
Quantum Synchronicity® Assessment
www.RuthKlein.com/Assessment

CHAPTER 4

QUANTUM SYNCHRONICITY® PRINCIPLE #1: THE SECRET ENERGY OF INTENTIONS

"Keep your thoughts on what you intend to create.
Stay consistently matched up with the field of intention,
and then watch for the clues that what you're summoning
from the all-creative Source is arriving in your life."
Dr. Wayne W. Dyer

Intentions help you to define and share your gifts, talents, and intellectual property while moving into your heartfelt desires and dreams. Intentions are the seed for creating your life. When this "seed" is paid attention to, nurtured, and appreciated, then you have set up the perfect environment for seeing the results your heart desires. If you continue to nurture them, pay attention to them, and appreciate them, they will grow and flourish as you allow the Universal Energy and Quantum Synchronicity® to handle all the details…just as you would in a beautiful vegetable garden. You wouldn't keep digging the dirt to check the eggplant seed to see if it's really an eggplant or to check how far it's gown. You just have a "knowing" that the eggplant seed will grow in the ground you've prepared. You plant it and then let go of the process and just keep watering and nurturing the plant. Even without "seeing" the eggplant vegetable, you "know" and act as if the eggplant will be seen in at the right time. You have planted the seed today for the future.

Intention is directly connected to your Spirit…that special place where you are brilliant and loving, and from where all your brilliant ideas come. Your Spirit ignites the spark of your dreams, your wishes, your hopes, and how you want to see and live in the world. And it is in this place of Authentic Truth where your ideas, inventions, and dreams begin to manifest in the physical world, as demonstrated in your work, career, relationships, money, love, and health.

How Are the Intentions of Generation Why Not?® Similar?

- Generation Why Not?® Intentions are based on their foundational values and beliefs.
- They are open to possibility.
- They believe anything is possible.
- They know they are co-creators with the Universe.

- They know that the Universal Laws are unbending, and they embrace them.
- They embrace the Universal Laws rather than resist them.
- They are careful and conscious not to create Paradoxical or competing Intentions.
- Their Intentions are based on abundance, not lack or fear.
- They are true to their word for themselves and others.
- Their words to themselves matter.
- They stay focused on their Intentions.
- They value clarity of purpose, clarity of their values, and clarity on the right actions.
- Their commitment to what they want and desire is greater than their commitment to fear.
- They listen to the wisdom of their Intuition.
- They are committed to the journey as much as they are to the outcome.
- They allow for the Universe to bring them results by being unattached to the specific outcome.

So much of Intention is "how" you go through it…your feelings, your state of Being, your attitude, and the energy of how you want your career and life to unfold. You may want to ask yourself throughout the day, "What is my Intention for this experience? What is my Intention for today? What is my Intention in the upcoming meeting?" Intentions allow you to "view" what's next. And the beauty is that you are the creator of what you want.

Intentions may take on the form of specific initiatives, as seen in Howard Schultz's *Onward: How Starbucks Fought for Its Life without Losing Its Soul.* As he elaborated on in his book, these initiatives are "Three Strategic Initiatives": "1) Improve the current state of its US retail business; 2) Reignite the emotional attachment with customers; and 3) Make long-term changes to the foundation of our business."

This is what Albert Einstein meant when he said, "Consciousness precedes all matter."

As Katherine Woodward Thomas noted in her book, *Calling in "The One"*: "We must believe in the possibility of a particular intention before it can come to us."

With the understanding of Quantum Physics and Synchronicity, you can start to see the intersection of Quantum Synchronicity® and how your consciousness, energy, and Intention are the powerful ingredients to success. What may seem like coincidences are actually energetic Synchronicity... connecting your energy vibration with that of the Universe's energy vibration. And we attract the energy vibration that we give out into the world, no matter what it is we *say* we want. It comes down to saying, thinking, intending, and living on a positive energy level *consistently* that attracts abundance. The Universe only knows Abundance!

Generation Why Notter David Meltzer, author, inspirational speaker, CEO of Sports 1 Marketing, who speaks with famous CEOs and high-visibility athletes and entrepreneurs all day long, says that: "I am focused on what I desire and want, rather than on what I don't want. And I do this by being very present to every decision, every phone call, and every contact I am involved in. I intend each of those experiences and how I would like them to go." He goes on to say, "Why would I not do that if I *know* that this makes the difference between success and not?"

What happens when your Intentions are not consistent and in alignment with your dreams and desires? The simple answer is that you attract the opposite of what you intend, and your Intentions become Paradoxical (competing) Intentions.

Paradoxical Intentions

On the average, we make 35,000 decisions daily. And many of these decisions are tinted with decisions we made between the ages of two and eight! Can you imagine making decisions with the cognitive skills of a two-, three-, or eight-year-old? And we are always making choices. What if we made choices to experience our activities and people with appreciation and trust, and be open to the possibility of reaching our dreams and goals? It all starts with Conscious Intention. Generation Why Notter Andrea Albright, whose online fitness, health, and lifestyle platform is valued at over $250 million says, "I am always in appreciation, even when things go wrong, because then I know that what I'm doing needs to be changed or tweaked. There's no downside to being in the state of appreciation all day long."

Since the Universe only knows Abundance, and successful manifestation requires the Universe's assistance, anything less than that is not on the same Universal channel. I learned this Law when I started working with computers and websites. If I didn't put the exact address into the browser, I wouldn't get the results I was looking for. One little letter misplaced or forgotten when emailing was all it took to take me off focus and out of alignment. No matter how much I may have "wished" for things to be different, it wasn't going to make a bit of difference. I had to follow the Law of the Computer! When I stopped getting upset and started accepting that this is just the way the Computer works, my life and research became much easier, and more importantly, I was getting the results I was looking for!!

It is the exact same situation with the Law of the Universe's Computer…the letters that this computer respond to are similar in nature to the Laws of the Universe, and they are a-p-p-r-e-c-i-a-t-i-o-n, g-r-a-t-i-t-u-d-e, l-o-v-e, p-o-s-i-t-i-v-i-t-y, a-c-c-e-p-t-a-n-c-e, t-r-u-s-t, n-o-n-a-t-t-a-c-h-m-e-n-t. Why do these words (Universal web addresses) work? Because these are the words that are in alignment with the Universal Laws of Abundance and high-level vibrational energy…the Universal web address to connect to Miracles and Manifestation.

The opposite happens when you worry, become anxious or fearful over your thoughts. If you are focused on these lower vibrational energies, then there is a very good chance that you will attract the very things you do not want. For example, if you are focused and worried about money and yet one of your Intentions is to Double Your Income, then you most likely will attract what you most fear…money leakages. Negative vibrations always drive away abundance and your Pure Intention. You end up manifesting the very opposite of what you Intend. This is what's called Paradoxical Intentions!

I remember when I used to get so nervous before speaking and, somewhere deep inside, I was thinking, *What if I forget to say something? What if I don't connect with my audience?* Well, I ended up receiving exactly what I was focusing on! I gave a speech to a large group. In fact, I believe I was given one of the largest spaces for my speech at a women's conference, which allowed a lot more people to hear me. I could feel I wasn't connecting with my audience and, worse yet, women began to leave!! My worst fears were unfolding right before me, and all I could do was think of how "everyone" was walking out, and all my fears and anxiety attracted ALL of it! But I didn't realize that at the time.

It was so traumatic for me that day that I decided not to be a public speaker for years! I didn't speak on the stage for several years until, one day, I realized a few things:

I was focusing on the very thing I feared would happen, and it reminded me that the Universal Laws are real, and they do work the same way each time. My fear was ego based…big time. I was worried about how the group would "judge" me. When I realized that I am speaking because I have a message I want to share—for whoever is in the audience—and it's not about me. When I realized that I was a messenger for the speech and it wasn't about me, I became a great, confident speaker.

To this day, I keep in mind those two things: focus on what I *do* want as I stay in alignment with the vibrational energy of my Conscious Intention as I speak, and whoever is in the audience is exactly who needs to be there at that moment. It's about their experience, not mine!

I experienced Paradoxical Intentions, up close and personal. I had given up my dream of being a keynote speaker by caving in to my fear, anxiety, and worry and, as a result, manifested the opposite of what I Intended! Here are some other Paradoxical Intentions (those thoughts that interfere with and cancel out the Intentions that you desire) that have shown up with my clients:

Intention: "I am going to attract $100,000 this year."

Paradoxical Intention: "I can't really make that kind of money. No one in my family has done that, so why do I think I can?"

Intention: "I'm going to save 10 percent of my income this year."

Paradoxical Intention: "I deserve to buy and have pretty things, as life is short."

Intention: "I am going to find the perfect business assistant for marketing."

Paradoxical Intention: "By the time I teach them what they need to know, I might as well do it myself."

Intention: "My Intention is to facilitate Millennials and Baby Boomers to be in harmony with each other."

Paradoxical Intention: "Those Millennials are so darn entitled. They expect everything to be handed to them."

By now, I'm sure you can see and understand why our Intentions may need to be focused on what we do want from what lies behind our true feelings of the situation, all driven by the subconscious. A very effective approach to "retrain" those aspects in your subconscious that lead to limitation is to start a bedtime ritual of Bedtime Intentions. Right before you go to bed, you say your positive and life-affirming Intentions in any area(s) of your life, and then allow the power of silence and sleep to marinate those future-oriented seeds.

Super Power in Bedtime Intentions

Bedtime is a very conducive time to Intend your desires and is an easy and simple process. Right before going to sleep, share a Bedtime Intention with the Universe as to what you desire, whether it be health, business related, relationships, or anything else, and then let it go. You have planted the seed, and your subconscious in partnership with the Universe will start the fundamental elements of manifestation. It is staying focused and in alignment with your deepest desires as you consciously co-create with the Universe in manifesting your desires in business and in your life.

You can say your Bedtime Intention out loud, quietly to yourself, or write it down...whichever way feels more powerful for you. Just remember to think Big! Here are the five steps I use for Bedtime Intentions:

1. Get relaxed and quiet your mind.
2. Thank the Universe for your Blessings of the day. You can always find something to be grateful for (e.g., breathing, being able to see, experiencing a sunset).
3. Ask your question or next steps in a relationship, something specific you're working on in business, a health question, or anything else that is on your mind and you would like some help with or insight into. You can also write down your Intention or say it out loud.

The more important part with Bedtime Intentions is to do them and do them consistently. You're speaking to the Universe and your subconscious to become loving bedfellows!

I use Bedtime Intentions for creating programs, live event titles, book ideas when I'm in the midst of writing a book, blog titles, new strategic options for clients, as well as helping me release any misunderstandings, judgments, or misidentifications that have kept me "hostage" with over-responsibility, self-judgment, or approval seeking.

Why Are Intentions So Important?

Working with entrepreneurs, CEOs, celebrities, and thought leaders, as well as my own experiences, I have found five important elements of Intention in attracting a successful business, relationship, or new life path: Intuition, Commitment, Clarity, Focus, and Momentum.

Intuition—Need to take time to listen to the small voice that is always there.

Commitment—Commitment to self and to your dreams/goals/purpose.

Clarity—Get clear on the big vision, your big "why" to keep moving you forward.

Focus—Allows you to stop the "monkey mind."

Momentum—The afterglow of the previous four elements brings you to action, and that action creates your momentum for your task or project at hand.

Intuition

Intuition is listening to that little voice inside that guides what you do. We all experience it, but few follow its guidance for our careers, relationships, and even our business's bottom line. In order to listen to that inner voice, we need to pause, be mindful, be present, and believe that what is being said to us is real and for our Higher Good. That's a tall order to follow at times, especially if there are things we are striving for or we're in a relationship that we really want to stay in...no matter what!

Intuition speaks the loudest when we are quiet. It is easy to drown out our Intuition with our fears, with other's opinions, and our own obsessive thoughts.

Interestingly enough, the majority of the people I interviewed for this book have a meditation practice and often comment on how vital meditation is to the fulfillment of their desires and dreams! Meditation is a consistent ritual, even if for only twenty minutes a day, although most of the Generation Why Not?® interviewees spent close to thirty minutes meditating daily.

Generation Why Notter Sandra Biskind, who is an author, speaker, and spiritual teacher, and has coached author Jack Canfield (and his team) of the *Chicken Soup for the Soul* books, and other high-profile transformational leaders in business, says: "I listened to that little voice inside that said that I was going to leave my boyfriend, my home, and my career to be with a man in another country! I knew from years earlier, that this little voice is my guide. Otherwise, there is no way I would have listened because on the outside it all looked ridiculous!" This is the beauty, as Sandra realized, in learning to flex your Intuition muscles. Once you have built up confidence in listening to previous intuitive messages and you felt it was the right thing to do for you, you are in a position to "believe" and/or listen to this inner guidance more often.

In the craze of so much "noise" in our environments, both externally and internally (thoughts), how do we find time to listen, be quiet, and take time out for ourselves daily?

All I can tell you is, if it's important enough to you, you will find a way! I've always loved the saying, "Where there's a will, there's a way." Generation Why Not?® pretty much lives by this saying. When one door closes, they look for the next door, a window, a peephole, or even a new location.

Plus, interestingly, if you do the following exercise below to help you "find" the time for meditating, it may help in answering a question, offering an insight that gives you clarity in that moment to help you move forward. You may be very surprised at what shows up for you.

The exercise is called a "Gestalt" exercise, in Psychology terms. You sit in a chair and have another chair face you (as though someone was sitting in it). The "second" chair (empty chair) is your Older, Wiser Self…or it could be Consciousness. Whatever you choose to call it, keep it consistent. The "second" chair may be your answer to finding the time for *you* to have that quiet time while being mindful and listening to what comes forward. It may seem simple, but its simplicity is its greatest gift and biggest impact!

Generation Why Notter Nick Taranto—Millennial, Cofounder of Plated, was on the television show, Shark Tank, and one of Forbes 30 Under 30, who sold his company to

Albertson's grocery company—says, "Meditation, when I remember to do it, is good for me, my partners, my stakeholders, my clients, and for my bottom line. It also calms me down. It allows me to quiet my mind and listen to my next steps."

It's important that you validate your own intuitive hits, rather than depending on others' opinions for validation. Why? Because you want to be a pure and clear vessel for you. Because, at the end of the day, only you are your best and most authentic co-creator.

We all have Intuition, but we sometimes have it blocked by the clouds of fear, anxiety, worry, or judgment.

I believe "listening" is an undervalued communication skill for ourselves, as well as for others. Often, when others are speaking, instead of really listening to them, in our own minds, we are preparing what we're going to say when their lips stop moving. Listening is that "small voice" that we all hear and choose to follow....or not. That small voice, most likely, is our wisdom... it's the place inside, if we stop to listen for it, that will guide us to make choices that fuel our career and relationship success. I often get the question, "Ruth, how do I know if it's my ego or really my Spirit talking?" The answer that I give is that the ego speaks from Fear, Self-Doubt, and Lack, whereas your Spirit speaks from Truth, Love, and Abundance.

Let's look at this a little closer in the following.

Commitment

Commitment pulls you through the times when you just "don't feel like doing it"—the "it" being anything. I find that commitment pulls me through and helps me be disciplined versus saying, "I don't FEEL like doing that now."

Since words matter, your word is gold. Commitment helps with keeping your word, committing to yourself, thus providing you with self-confidence and self-integrity that, when you say you are going to do something, you can depend on yourself and you do it. It adds a level of self-trust and makes you trustworthy to yourself and to others! Somewhere along the line, you have made a decision, and your commitment to that decision is priceless.

Creating an Intention is making a commitment to yourself. It is your way of engaging and being in full alignment with who you are and what you stand for. It offers you self-integrity, and you commit to your decision, whatever it takes.

Integrity

We often hear of self-integrity, but what does that really mean in the landscape of everyday living and everyday business? Even though the meaning seems self-evident, when you really look at this concept closer and deeper, you may realize that this is an area that is often bypassed due to lack of discipline, lack of focus, lack of direction, lack of clarity, lack of boundaries…always looking outside of us to be integrous in our business. But what about being integrous within ourselves?

When you make the commitment that your word is gold… it helps you keep your promises to yourself, thus providing you with self-confidence and self-integrity that, when you say you are going to do something, you do…adds another deep level of self-trust!!!!

We know that, if we don't have integrity with others in business, we will most likely lose our jobs and, if we own the company, our Brand will be tarnished. And, in today's social media and word-of-mouth digital world, that could be worth tens of thousands or millions of lost dollars to you and your business, let alone your self-confidence.

But what about the times we have told ourselves that we will be doing something, and it is often the first thing to go by the wayside if we're busy, as in exercising more, taking our supplements, making X amount of business development calls, or following up as we have planned on our to-do list: waking up earlier to meditate and a myriad of "I am going to…." This often leads to a short trek, a false beginning, or forgetting entirely about what we said we would do for ourselves.

Why is that? There are a number of reasons, but, at the end of the day, if we continue to say we will do something for ourselves and we don't, then, many times, it can be a reflection of our self-worth. Or perhaps there's resistance somewhere else? Is it possible that we may feel less valuable than someone else? Since our subconscious is the real driver in our actions, what may be lurking in those "hidden" crevices?

Do we truly not have the time that is necessary to follow up on our own word to ourselves? If something is really important to you, do you make the time to do it? If something is really valuable to you, do you do what it takes to take care of it?

I really value my health, and yet I was not going to a Zumba class I love because it is scheduled for midmorning and, instead, I would keep working for many weeks and then months, and only go sporadically. Why is that? Once I realized that I was feeling frustrated with myself for putting exercise I really enjoyed on hold and working through those two mornings a week, I realized that I could not trust myself to follow up on what I said I would do for myself. That was not a good feeling, and yet I knew it was the truth.

The deeper I went into this resistance, I realized that, years ago, I experienced a situation where I tried every option available to me. This lasted for several years and, at the end of the day, the proverbial "sh**" hit the fan anyway. I evidently made an "unconscious" decision at that time, that: "Whatever I do, it doesn't really matter. Things are going to happen, and I can't control them, so why really spend a lot of my energy on them?" And I ended up "showing up" by putting things off that I said I would do for myself, like taking supplements consistently, exercising an hour a day, completing different projects, and the list goes on. Once I realized that this is the way I was showing up 20 percent of the time, I quickly turned things around, because not being able to trust myself to get something done that I said I would do for myself was baffling, confusing, and very frustrating!

I have learned that the way you show up in one part of your life is most likely how you show up in other parts of your life. And I find that how you show up is tied to "your story," whether it is focused on abundance or lack. Looking through the lens of abundance sees the glass at least half full and is powered by staying open to possibility and openness; and looking through the lens of lack sees the glass less than half empty and is powered by fear or past experiences we've interpreted as traumatic or "awful."

Generation Why Notter Chris Draft, whom my daughter affectionately calls Draftie, is an NFL Ambassador and former NFL linebacker, International Cancer Advocate, and president of the Chris Draft Family Foundation. He is committed to making a difference in the lives of people with cancer, even though—or because—his wife died of lung cancer. His Intention is to use the power of the NFL platform, which he knew intimately, to make a disruptive change in the minds of people around cancer: what it means, how it's measured, how it affects people as well as the community, and what each one of us can do to make a positive difference in our lives, in our communities, and with those who have cancer.

Chris is now making a difference off the field, just as he made a difference on the gridiron with his teammates. What we don't realize sometimes is that life waits for no one, and, as Chris says, "Cancer provides urgency." What if we had that same "urgency" in living a life tied to our commitment and our Conscious Intentions?

Generation Why Not?® makes commitments and they stick to them, no matter what. And, if they find this not to be true, they know how to turn the tide. Chris Draft says he tells people to "Bring Your Socks On," intentionally looking at your feet and toes. Why is that important? Because to put your socks on is to pay attention to the little details. Chris says, "It's important to put your attention on the details; details matter and they have consequences. As a professional athlete, playing and competing at the highest level, the details matter. And, if your socks or shoes are not on perfectly, then that can cost you a game."

When we speak of a new possibility for ourselves such as, "I'm committed to having an extraordinary relationship," then all kinds of amazing coincidences, unforeseen opportunities, and unpredictable synchronicities are put into motion. That is why it is so important to have integrity with our word. It trains the Universe to take us seriously.

Hence, Quantum…a little each day and with consistency of thoughts, words, and action…unforeseen Synchronicities show up!

How Do You Show Up in the World?

How you show up in the world is a direct reflection of your self-integrity…how you have committed to living your life. Not just in one area, but in all areas of your life. I have often wondered if people who go through tough times show up differently than when times are good in their lives. My observation and experience tell me that you are you, no matter what.

Sandra Biskind believes "the way you show up in the world is pivotal to your success in business and in life." Sandra created a multimillion-dollar business and then lost it all. In fact, she owed money to many vendors. She found she was not in a good mood and then realized that how she showed up during this time in her life, as well as with her vendors, would make a difference. She changed her attitude, her state of Being, as she went through the financial devastation. Her Intention was to pay everyone back, but not right away. She needed time to regain her footing. To her amazement, her vendors allowed her to have outstanding debt while she got back on her feet.

She eventually paid off each person and, afterward, their business relationship lasted for years.

Clarity

I used to undervalue clarity. I remember being in a workshop and the mentor was spending much of the time about "clarity." In fact, she said that "clarity is worth tens of thousands of dollars." At the time, I didn't fully understand what she was saying. Years later, I completely get what she meant. Here is a sampling:

- Getting clarity around my business model afforded me the ability to focus on how I truly wanted to run my business that was in alignment with me and my Personal Brand.
- Getting clarity for the marketing strategies that work best for me allowed me to stop money leakage by not spending money on marketing strategies that didn't work…even though they may have worked for others.
- Getting clarity about my team's motivation and what drives them in my business allowed me to give them more challenging work in their areas of interest and talent.
- Getting clarity about my Business Brand gave me permission to be myself and showed me how what I bring to my clients is unique and of value.
- Getting clarity about my ideal client afforded me a financially rich and purpose-driven business.

David Meltzer says: "Creating relationship capital and learning how to leverage it is important in all businesses and life. Half of my business value is derived from this asset I call relationship capital. Networking works. Who you know matters more than what you know. It exposes and attracts opportunities."

Clarity pulls you through the times when you just "don't feel like doing it." It pulls you through and helps you with discipline versus "I don't FEEL like doing that now."

What Is Your Intention for Your Business and Brand?

A big part of your Business Brand is the experience that your clients have before working with you, while working with you, and after working with you. It is the experience that they enjoy, and it is important for that experience to be consistent each time you have a "touch point" with them (e.g., newsletters, social media, blog posts, speeches, delivery of services and/or products, follow-up, and payment structure).

There's a wonderful book entitled *The McKinsey Way,* by author Ethan Rasiel. Despite various views of McKinsey over the years, the core Intention of the Brand that founder James "Mac" McKinsey and his partner, Marvin Bower, set out to build their company around speaks volumes of their vision. The company takes a full day off with its entire global workforce every year just to review the company's values. Think of how much the company is investing just in the Intention of their Brand? Not surprisingly, McKinsey is known as a "CEO Factory," as many of its consultants go on to run large companies.

I would like to share some insights into the McKinsey Intention of their Brand by author Ethan Rasiel. Since McKinsey likes to come up with an Initial Hypothesis during the first visit on a consulting project, here is what Rasiel refers to as a Business Intention for the company that they use for each project that is value based and consistent:

- Understanding the "right" problem is the key.
- Don't reinvent the wheel. Every problem will be similar to another but, at the same time, unique.
- Don't make facts fit into your solution.
- Make sure the solution fits for your client. (A wonderful business solution is useless if the company lacks the resources to follow the advice.)
- Sometimes problems may be unsolvable, so suggest alternatives.

I personally love these value-based Intentions for the international consulting firm, McKinsey.

I leave you with, "What are your top five Business Values and Intentions?" And one more thing: just as you would create an Intention for your Business, there are others who create an Intention during the last part of their lives. Chris Draft met a feisty, redheaded woman who wanted to hug everyone she met at the Super Bowl, and she did. Her battle with lung cancer ended shortly after she manifested her Intention!

Focus

Generation Why Notter Dr. David Carter, Dean, M.A. in Ethical Leadership and TEDx speaker, said his Intention was to always teach. That is the one thing he focused on. He says, "Everyone is a genius." Dr. Carter believes that effective leadership requires the Intention of humility and collaboration.

Your Intentions direct both your energy and consciousness and, as such, create the focus of your business and life goals. Your Intentions will direct the bountiful Universe to assist you in every way possible, so keeping them focused on your desires is profoundly important.

David Klein, Generation Why Notter, co-founder and CEO of CommonBond, a fintech (financial technology) company valued at hundreds of millions of dollars, says: "I went to business school with the express purpose of starting a company upon graduating. I wanted to build a great company with lasting impact."

Momentum

The more time you think about your Priority Intentions and your daily Intentions, the more clarity and momentum you create. In other words, what is your objective in these situations and what results do you intend to manifest? What manifests in the future is what you intend today—now!

Momentum is about engaging and re-engaging in many different areas. For example, when you feel "plugged in" to a group of friends, you have a certain feeling of engagement. However, if you haven't been in touch with them for a while, you may still like them, but you're now unplugged from the group energy.

This happens in business all the time. In fact, one of the biggest challenges CEOs and founders find is that they need to be alert and filled with momentum in order to grow and scale up. This requires engagement and re-engagement between themselves, their clients, and their employees. This is a very important point to consider when you're in business. Think about it for a moment…your employees, vendors, partners, clients, and stakeholders want to hear from you and want to feel they matter. One of the best ways to help someone feel that they are important to the company is engaging with them. This is particularly important if the employees feel engaged, plugged in…connected to the company's mission. And this engagement is what has lifted social media to be the driving force it is today.

I suggest you create three strategies that help you to engage and re-engage with all your stakeholders to keep up the momentum for yourself and for your business.

Four Steps to Creating Powerful Conscious Intentions

There are four steps in manifesting your heart's desire for a business meeting, a project, a conversation, an athletic event, or whatever it is you want to manifest.

1. **Think It! Thoughts**

   First of all, know that Quantum Synchronicity® exists and is real. Just being open to Possibility allows you the freedom to "see" outside your blind spots.

2. **Speak It! Words**

   We speak the word, and then we let it go—trusting that, as we do our best to live congruently with the Intention we set, whatever happens is perfect. Words are important! Speaking what it is that we are committed to creating.

3. **Believe It! Visualization**

   Being able to "see" it and "feel" it as if it were already here and real. So many of the Generation Why Not?® people I interviewed use Visualization as an important and vital step in manifesting their heart's desires in all types of situations! Why? Because visualizing what you desire as already happening with emotion activates your brain's reticular activating system (RAS). Why is this important? Because one of its functions in the brain is to control consciousness.

4. **Live It! Action without Attachment to Results**

   This may be the most difficult step, as it requires you to completely surrender any attachment to the outcome you are committed to creating. It is about staying focused on your Intention, while still letting go of specific results.

It is this energy Consciousness that is the first seed of seeing tangible results in our physical world, but all things start from this seed of energy consciousness…every invention, every idea, every situation we see played out in our lives, physically, personally, relationally. And why is this possible? We now know through Quantum Physics that, if our thoughts are energy and energy is matter, then we go from energy to matter in everything we create in our Consciousness.

Now, I ask you to look at the next few months (and certainly you can do this on a much longer scale) and create Your Business Strategy Intention.

Intention is the seed where all of manifestation is created. Intention is connected to a bigger purpose of who we are and what we do, and is directly related to our Spirit and our talents.

Here's a way to get in touch with that higher purpose Intention for your Business and Brand:

1. Stop, pause, and just quiet the mind for a few minutes.
2. Ask the question: "What is the best use of my talents and time in the next ninety days for my business?"
3. Here are some possible ideas of what clients have shared over the years:

    Realtor: "My Intention is to be a blessing to everyone I meet today."
    Lawyer: "My Intention is to reconnect with all my active clients just to lessen the anxieties concerning their cases."

Coach: "My Intention is to connect and reconnect with all the people I have met within the last six months."

Speaker: "My Intention is to inspire women to reconnect to their Feminine Divinity."

Financial Planner: "My Intention is to be a money partner with my clients as though it were my money being invested."

Author: "My Intention is to zone out and write four hours a day with Grace and Ease."

My Priority Intention (Ruth): "My Intention is to live in the Miracle Field...living in Gratitude, always staying open to possibilities and asking, 'Why Not?'"

And...

"My Intention is to see every day as a Bonus!"

Here are some ideas for Intentions in other areas of your life.

Home Intentions:

"My Intention is to keep my dishes washed and clothes put away every day."

"My Intention is to have a loving and peaceful home to come home to."

"My Intention is to keep calm when the children are crying, screaming, arguing with each other."

Personal Intentions:

"My Intention is to stay open to opinions that differ
   from mine."
"My Intention is to be Present and observe my thoughts and
   the words I use with myself and others."
"My Intention is to accept "What is" today.

Love Relationship Intentions:

"My Intention is to take my time to get to know this
   lovely person."
"My Intention is to clarify and ask questions to better under-
   stand what the other person is really saying."
"My Intention is to attract my loving match into my life."
"My Intention is to see my beloved through Heart-
   Centered Eyes."

Parental Relationship:

"My Intention is to really listen before speaking today."
"My Intention is to stay open to whatever is said or done."
"My Intention is to stay in the Loving, no matter what."

Intention Tips:

- Plant the seed of your heart's desire with your Intention.
- Your Intention is part of your big Why.

- Everything you do is Intentional.
- Every Intention lies through the lens of your perception of self-confidence.

Realignment Tip:

- The moment you feel or think something is not correct, believe it!

Generation Why Not?®
Breakthrough Bonus Download #1
Morning and Bedtime Intention Template
Bonus download here:
www.RuthKlein.com/why-not-bonuses

Meditation on Creating Powerful Intentions
Listen to it here: www.ruthklein.com/why-not-bonuses

Song that captures the essence of the chapter:
"Make Your Own Kind of Music" by Mama Cass Elliot

CHAPTER 5

QUANTUM SYNCHRONICITY®
PRINCIPLE #2:
THE SECRET ENERGY OF THOUGHTS

*"The intuitive mind is a sacred gift and the
rational mind is a faithful servant. We have created a society
that honors the servant and has forgotten the gift."*
Albert Einstein

Thoughts are the second principle in Quantum Synchro-nicity®. Your thoughts and ideas create your reality and how you live and see the world. Quantum Synchronicity® maintains that ideas, dreams, and thoughts are factual, first existing in a powerful reality that you don't visually see—at least, not at first.

Thoughts are incredibly powerful because they are a combination of your mental and emotional energy! The more energy in the form of feelings that are attached to a thought, the stronger the vibrational pull is to that energy. Your business and your life move in the direction of your most powerful thought patterns. That is why our thoughts govern our lives. If you want to change your life, you must first change your thoughts!

Albert Einstein recognized the vital importance of being able to envision things, stressing: "Imagination is more important than knowledge. For knowledge is limited, whereas imagination embraces the entire world, stimulating progress, giving birth to evolution." In addition, Einstein said, "Everything in life is vibrations."

Another renowned physicist, Nikola Tesla, advised, "If you want to find the secrets of the Universe, think in terms of energy, frequency, and vibrations."

Quantum Physics tells us that vibrational energy or thought is what creates matter, what we can see and touch. A popular proverb that has long described a related phenomenon is "mind over matter." This is how the energy of thoughts creates your world in many ways, a self-fulfilling prophecy. We can create things and make them happen and manifest in our lives by embracing this energetic and vibrational thought process.

Generation Why Not?® has harnessed the importance and awareness of being open to possibilities of doing things and thinking of ways that are different from the status quo or, in some cases, conventional wisdom—and even staying open to hear others' diverse options, without judgment. It is this creation of a "can do" attitude, possibility mindset, and state of Being that aligns this Generation with the Universal Laws of Quantum Synchronicity®. And, as a result, they share this paradigm thought shift in their business and in their lives. The same Quantum Synchronicity® principles work for attracting love relationships as they do in your business. Why is this? Because attracting what you desire, as many have called the Law of Desire, works Universally…just as the Law of Gravity works Universally, no matter who you are, what you do, or what year you were born.

In addition to thought vibrations, our emotions are generated by our thoughts! That is good news. Why? Because we can create positive results and life-serving emotions just as easily as we create negative emotions. I'll be sharing more on this later in the chapter. In the meantime, just know that, when you change your thoughts, you change your emotions! And, when you change your thoughts and accompanying emotions, you can change your business, your communications, your health, and your relationships in the direction you desire.

Neutral Observation

Thoughts are incredibly powerful, as they are the source of your mental and emotional energy. Thoughts without "charged" emotions are what I like to call "neutral observation" or "neutral curiosity."

A very powerful strategy I have used over the years is to be in this "observation mode" during the day. I consciously observe my thoughts and focus on being "neutral" when things occur, or when I would normally have thoughts of rushing, overwhelm, or frustration, or when I'm too attached to the results. Being neutral is a skill in remembering to not judge your thoughts as good or bad, or what you think the situation, person, or behavior "should" do or be. Rather, you are in observation mode and appreciating the experience, which automatically puts you in a high vibrational energy of gratitude.

Thoughts, in their purest form, are neutral. How we interpret or judge our thoughts shapes our emotions around the ideas, and then our thoughts are "charged," either positively or negatively. This became so apparent to me years ago when one of my sons, David, fell into a swimming pool when he was only eighteen months old. His father was right in front of him, as David was sitting on the edge of the pool. In the corner of my eye, I saw David fall into the pool and immediately told his dad to fetch him. When the baby came out of the water, he didn't know what to think. He looked around to see what just happened. Even though his dad and I were nervous, we smiled and laughed, and then David followed suit. So much of our early thoughts are environmentally influenced by others. And, as a result, many times we immediately go into an emotional state of feeling up or down because of habit. Generation Why Not?® has taken quiet time to pause at some point to focus on what makes them tick… what creates enjoyment and positive flow, what creates stagnation and a feeling of just surviving, rather than thriving.

Are Your Thoughts Important to Your Quality of Life?

As mentioned, our thoughts have a cognitive power that gives off vibrational energy and accompanying messages within our energetic field. Thoughts are either positive or negative—positive thoughts attract higher vibrational energy, while negative thoughts attract lower vibrational energy. You can actually "feel" your energy in both of these instances. When you're feeling upbeat and positive, you are usually feeling good and joyful, and your day is going well. The opposite is true when you're feeling down.

Much of the way we are feeling is directly related to what we are thinking. Your thoughts literally control your day, and *you* control your thoughts! So, if you want to move forward in achieving your goals and your definition of success, you will want to be a Conscious Thinker. In fact, the moment you experience an energy drain, here are three things you can do immediately to identify and hopefully convert the drain into energy:

1. Identify the emotions you're feeling (you will find a list of emotions in the online Bonus Download (www. RuthKlein.com/why-not-bonuses).

2. Scan your thoughts to identify what you're telling yourself, what you're thinking—the actual words you're saying to yourself. Our emotions are closely tied to our thoughts/internal words we tell ourselves, and our thoughts fuel our emotions.

3. Think of a more positive way to interpret what you're thinking. Can you "reframe" your thoughts/words to something more neutral and without a negative emotional charge?

Seven Thought Patterns That Block Our Success

Thought patterns are ways in which we think and, in some cases, an obsessive type of thinking about certain things. Another name for this would be a "thought habit."

The focus of your most dominant thoughts right now and the energy of these thoughts are most likely automatic and habitual. Unless we are conscious of our thoughts, the resulting emotions attract the same Vibrational Energy Field back to you. One constant business thought throughout the day can be fear! And fear begets more fear, unless you consciously stop the obsessive thinking. The very thinking you don't want to happen. For example, a client of mine was very fearful of giving speeches. As a result, she said "no" to every speaking opportunity. She knew that, once she launched her new book, she would need to give speeches to sell books. As we worked together, the thoughts that created the emotions of fear for her were coming from long ago. She kept "hearing" her mom's unsupportive words to her. She had internalized these thoughts about herself for over fifty years! Once we worked together on her misidentified thoughts, we were able to create an awesome speech that has her audiences laughing, crying, and buying books. Her speech reflects who she is today: a strong woman who knows her value and is reaching out to be of service to women through her books and speeches.

The power of your most dominant thoughts vis-à-vis the strength or force of your emotions aligns with your personal energy field. This vibration sends out signals within and outside of you as to what is attracted into your life. The good news is that, if you're unhappy with where you are now, either professionally or personally, you can turn it around immediately! Changing your thoughts will change the intensity of your emotions and the energy you draw to yourself. Generation Why Not?® is able to turn around what they're thinking and the accompanying emotions quicker than most.

So much of our fear can be turned into taking action. As Nike's famous advertising slogan urges: "Just Do It." My mantra that I have used for myself and my clients for decades is: "Just Start It!" Fear rests in thoughts, while curiosity takes us toward possibility, with action taking us out of our torrential, obsessive thinking. As Einstein rather pithily put it, "I have no special talent. I am only passionately curious."

Generation Why Not?® uses two skills to move them out of negativity. One is that they have a keen and strong focus on moving forward in their businesses. Secondly, they are always looking for a new way, a new option…other possibilities in solving problems, creating new programs, and innovating from scratch! The more "stuck" we are, the more we hook up to fear, rather than curiosity or being open to possibilities.

Fear causes a whole host of things to happen in your business and in your life, many of which you don't want. However, the very idea of fear runs deeply and shows up in many ways. I would like to share seven Thought Patterns of Fear and how they can easily derail your efforts and your success.

Fear Thought Pattern #1: Anxiety

Anxiety rears its head when we start to think "too much." We literally stop ourselves…a thought paralysis of confusion. Anxiety shows up when we find ourselves in indecision because we're afraid that we might make the wrong decision, so our thoughts stay in indecision. David Klein, CEO of CommonBond, says: "You've got to make good decisions quickly. You usually have enough information to make these decisions quickly, as long as you don't start to doubt them. When indecision surfaces, confusion is triggered, and an important opportunity is oftentimes missed."

Disruptive Thought Paradigm Shift:
"I have enough information to make a decision or take action now. I can always tweak, if I need to."

Fear Thought Pattern #2: Worry

Worry keeps us up at night thinking "What if?" questions... What if I fail? What if this project fails? What if I run out of money? These "What if?" questions that keep us up at night are about trying to figure out the future, right now. Rather than be in the present and know that you have always done or taken action that was required of you when it was needed will help to thwart these "What if?" worry questions that can stop you in your tracks, keeping you from taking action or staying open to possibilities and the creativity that is needed in making out-of-the-box decisions.

Disruptive Thought Paradigm Shift:
"I choose to take one small step, as I know action

alleviates worry. And I know 96 percent of
all worries never come to fruition."

Fear Thought Pattern #3: Control

Control is said to be the master of all addictions! There is a certain amount of truth that says you are the one who knows the best thing for your business...up to a point! Chances are you are the visionary who started your business or effectively turned around a department. However, at some point, the reins of control no longer belong to you...or, at least, not to you alone. When you are the visionary and creator of your business, you need to realize that control will only keep you small, as it is not a prescription for growth. Why? Because there is only one of you and, as you grow, you must open yourself and your mind to the creativity and guidance and skills of others and brainstorm together, making decisions based on old and new material presented. The pull to control is the strongest, I have learned, from those who have difficulty staying open to hearing many different thoughts and easily close down when they hear things they don't immediately agree with. In other words, they are quick to judge others' comments and ideas as "Not good," "That won't work here," "We've already tried that," and similar closed-minded thinking. Not that this is a bad thing; it simply represents a form of the fear of having others take control of your "baby."

Disruptive Thought Paradigm Shift:
"Staying open to others' perceptions, particularly

> *if they're different than mine, opens up*
> *new possibilities in my business."*

Fear Thought Pattern #4: Reverse Delegation

Reverse Delegation is the cousin to control. This is where the very people that you've hired to help you end up learning to check everything with you before making their final decision or complete what they're working on. This is usually the result of employees' fear that they will "get in trouble," or "be yelled at for not doing exactly what you want them to do," or they have learned that, if they don't complete something in a timely fashion, you or someone else will complete it. I see this happening in large companies, although it also happens in much smaller businesses as well.

> *Disruptive Thought Paradigm Shift:*
> *"I am allowing the people I've hired to be competent at*
> *what they were hired to do, as it leaves me open to expand*
> *and get more accomplished and be more productive."*

Fear Thought Pattern #5: Fear of Failure—Self-Doubt

Fear of Failure is what I refer to as the path of least resistance. This fear of not succeeding is so great that the subconscious (the subconscious is what drives our behavior, not our conscious selves) impels the behavior, and often it shows up as procrastination, lack of follow-up, a late start for a project, and time stress on an undertaking. At the end of the day, the person whose thought pattern is fear of failure can say, "I didn't have enough time," or some other "excuse" outside of themselves for not completing the project.

Disruptive Thought Paradigm Shift:
"I know much more than I realize, and I am
talented and resourceful. I can do this."

Fear Thought Pattern #6: Fear of Success

Fear of Success is also an interesting thought pattern. I have found, over the years working with clients and doing research on this topic, that the dominant thought here is that the person does not feel they deserve to be successful. You can find this thought pattern in the most talented and skilled people.

Another part of fear of success may come from the feeling that the more success they have, the more pressure they have to keep performing and make every project a successful hit. This thought pattern can add a lot of undue pressure and stress on the person. And, if the person doesn't keep up the high grade, then there's room to fall and, with it, their self-confidence.

Ultimately, it shows up as paralysis…no action.

Disruptive Thought Paradigm Shift:
"I take action every day and do the best I can, as I
know it will all fall into place…eventually."

Fear Thought Pattern #7: Doing Versus Being

Many businesses and entrepreneurs strongly believe they must be doing something all the time, not letting up, or the company will go down in some way. These CEOs and entrepreneurs find themselves exhausted and burned out, all the while working in their businesses, taking meetings, and doing the myriad of tasks necessary to run a successful and thriving business. If you suggest to them that they take an afternoon off or take a long lunch, they look at you quizzically as though you don't understand the many pressures and tasks they have going on. This may go on at this level of intensity for years! The idea of just Being and not Doing is a foreign concept.

You may also find this thought pattern brings a lot of time stress and rushing around.

> *Disruptive Thought Paradigm Shift:*
> *"I have the time to plan to do all that I need to do today."*

Who Do You Think You Are?

Mike, a leadership coach, wanted to break out and begin a coaching program and tried for over three years to publish his leadership book. After working with him a few weeks, it became evident that Mike had deep-seated doubts that said, "Who do you think you are?" "You won't be successful, so why even try?" At a young age, Mike "misinterpreted" what was going on and being said by people in his immediate family. And he internalized these remarks, that actually had nothing to do with him but were said to him by a parent, and he lived out those "words," deciding at a young age that that was who he truly was. Since our subconscious drives our thoughts and beliefs, his willpower to change and move forward only lasted a short time. By the way, this is what happens to many people with New Year's resolutions that are based on willpower to change. It rarely works…just ask gym membership directors and weight loss centers.

Mike consciously tried to make changes. He was able to do this, but he felt he was going uphill the entire way. Just as he hit a certain point, he plateaued, and then nothing more happened. We all have what I call a "set point"—a point in which we have given ourselves permission to think a certain way about ourselves and the success that we can envision, which also includes the amount of money we can earn.

Speaking a New Language

Since our thoughts and emotions directly influence our energy, and this directly influences our success, then being open to the possibility of a new language may be a good thing. Sending out negative or hostile energy to others or yourself (through self-criticism and self-rejection) only resends this energy back to you, so, in the meantime, the boomerang effect of this negativity kicks up obstacles to your pursuit of success. And, in this self-defeating cycle of fear, doubt, judgment, and attachment, you find yourself enjoying far less of what you're doing every day, until nothing seems to be good enough or special enough to make you happy, joyful, or feeling peaceful.

The new language consists of knowing that *words matter!* Words are a direct outcome of our thoughts and the intensity of our emotions! If you're doubting what you want others to do at work or thinking in a self-doubting way, these thoughts will directly impact how you come across to the other person or affect you personally.

For example, a book author continually said to herself and others that "I wish my book was more successful." Here are the facts:

- She had just come off a book launch and received best-selling positioning in two categories, one being a very competitive one.
- Her book sold over 1,000 books on Amazon, on her book tours, and speaking gigs within nine months of its release. And more books were sold in bookstores.
- She was getting people to ask her to speak.
- She was getting media exposure on television shows with millions of viewers.
- She had a speech that converted into books being bought and new speaking opportunities.

Here is what a Perceptual Thought Shift would sound like: "My book launch was very successful, and I am grateful to be selling more and more books with all the marketing and speaking opportunities that come before me." An old thought pattern for this author was "self-doubt" and "Things don't work out for me." You can see that the old thought patterns restricted and slowed down the very results she wanted!

What we commit to doing and the words we use in our agreements to ourselves and others do matter. In fact, one of the best strategies to build self-confidence, self-empowerment, and self-trust is to follow up with the agreements and commitments that you make to yourself, specifically, and to others. It is difficult to move forward on your dreams when you aren't sure if you're going to be true to yourself and follow up. I experienced this conundrum for several years after my divorce, ending a marriage of thirty-plus years, when I felt that everything I knew to be true no longer was. It took me a few years to stop wobbling and get my footing. In that time, as I was finding my legs again to stand upright without swaying with the wind, I found myself making all these agreements and commitments to myself, and barely following up on most of them. I am grateful that I had a beautiful and successful career, and I put every ounce of energy I had into my career. However, my focused energy on my business was about 50 percent of what I had been doing beforehand. I would go out of my way to fulfill my commitments to others and would feel exhausted a few hours into the day. I had never experienced this type of energy drain in my life. I was so energetically and emotionally depleted that my thyroid gave out because of all the anxiety, overwhelm, and disorientation I felt daily. And here's the truth: My thoughts, words, and interpretation of what I perceived to be "happening" outside of me fueled my lack of energy and thyroid issues. For years, I tried to "will" my agreements with myself so that I could fully trust myself and follow up with what I said I would do. It took a full three years before I could start to trust myself in doing what I said I would do for me. Even then, I was only fully engaged 80 percent of the time.

I have learned, finally, to realize that this, too, will pass and it will all work out well. In fact, my experience has consistently been that it normally works out even better than I could have imagined. My new mantra is: "I don't have to worry." When I look back at all the times I worried and lost sleep over things, I always end up saying to myself, "I never had to worry." The newer mantra reminds me to stay balanced and avoid obsessive worrying, which only makes matters worse by draining energy, focus, and motivation.

Eleven Vibrational Intentional Thoughts of Generation Why Not®?

Through my research, interviews, and clients' experiences, I have found there are eleven common vibrational thoughts within Generation Why Not?®. I will list what these are here and, throughout the book, share how the people in Generation Why Not?® express and live from these higher vibrational thought frequencies. For now, I will just say that "Living in the Miracle Field" is accepting "What Is," and this allows you to be open to options and possibilities.

1. Giving up is not an option.
2. Failure is only feedback for learning.
3. Everything is "feedback."

4. They guard their thoughts and know ways to prevent going down the rabbit hole of doubt.
5. They often ask themselves, "What's the best use of my time right now?"
6. They stay in motion to utilize momentum.
7. Adversity makes them stronger and doesn't define them.
8. They are driven by self-mastery leadership.
9. They always ask in one way or another, "Why Not?"
10. They stay committed to their word, to themselves, and to others.

Thoughts can be an expense for you or an investment in your potential, in your business, in your relationships, and in your health.

Case Study: Getting Stuck

The way you see yourself is how you tell yourself who you are. And how you see yourself is what you expect of yourself. If you tell yourself you're a loser and can't make things work, then that is exactly what you'll expect of yourself and that's what you'll receive in most situations.

Your attitude regarding failure feeds what you continue to think about yourself. It becomes a self-fulfilling prophecy. This type of thinking produces very low energy, and, in turn, you have now magnetically connected to the same low Universal vibrational force.

For example, Suzanne, a forty-something attorney, came to see me because she didn't know if she should go into private practice or work for someone else's law firm.

The Challenge: To go into private practice or work at someone else's law firm?

The Real Issue: These were some of Suzanne's thoughts that kept her not only indecisive, but also from moving forward in her career.

- "I don't know if I can be successful on my own."
- "What if I fail at this? Then my family suffers financially."
- "I don't deserve to be wealthy."
- "I haven't had much financial success in my life."
- I'm never going to make the money I want."

Disruptive Intervention: What needs to happen here with Suzanne, so she can move forward in her career?

First, it was important to uncover what she was telling herself. Words *do* matter! However, it's difficult to catch our thoughts as we tell them to ourselves.

Second, I had her put a checkmark on a piece of paper every time she said the "should" word. The self-critical part of her was always pushing her to do those "shoulds."

Third, it was important to ask her whose voice(s) she heard when she was telling herself those things.

Fourth, it was important to identify the first time that she could remember that she didn't feel successful or that she felt not good enough.

Fifth, we then started to review and "check out" the truth of where and how those thoughts came about.

When Suzanne was ready to create new thoughts, using new high vibrational words, she was able to rewrite a new story of who she was today. She was also able to build her self-confidence with truthful statements that she could now find support for, from previous successful experiences. The statement "Your net worth is directly related to your self-worth" rears its head often in my consulting and coaching practice.

Disruptive Paradigm Shift: Learn new ways of seeing the truth about her present life and what she has already accomplished. To become conscious of what she was thinking daily and writing it all down, and then changing those thoughts to what the truth is for her today.

Suzanne saw that she was passionate about her field of law and that she was very successful in helping her clients who needed an advocate. She realized that she'd been an advocate for children for decades. Once she was able to "see" herself as she truly was and identify the old thought messages that were created by old beliefs from other family members, she was able to lift her vibrational frequency to truth, rather than stay stuck in fear and limitation.

Results: Suzanne opened up her own practice five years ago, and as of this writing, she is financially taking care of her family and loves what she does! An added benefit is that she now employs several legal assistants.

Quantum Physics shows us that Thoughts start out as small vibrational energy (can't see it...physics calls it nonmaterial) and then, miraculously, the thoughts you couldn't initially see become evident by what shows up in your life (material matter), all originating from your nonvisible thoughts.

Thought vibrational energy (Quantum Physics) is very powerful, not only to yourself, but to everyone around you. Whatever energy vibration you are emitting is the energy that will harmonize with other energies—this is what you'll receive in kind. You can feel it when things are going well, and you feel on top of the world…you think you can accomplish anything at this level of energy. And the opposite is just as true when you're feeling energetically drained and upset.

This is why it's important to stay conscious as to the positive energy or negative energy that you're producing. You are a twenty-four-hour energy-production plant. And you can change the direction of this energy at any moment. Generation Why Not?® has the same up and down days as everyone else. However, they have learned to stay very conscious to this energy and Intention.

Generation Why Notter David Meltzer, Executive Business Coach, Keynote Speaker, and CEO and Co-Founder of Sports 1 Marketing.

Challenge: Pull out of bankruptcy.

Issue: He said that he thought his ego outpaced everything he did. He was making a lot of money and had a lot of man-toys, but his marriage was falling apart, and he felt completely unhappy and lost. Meltzer says, "At the peak of my financial success I was lost. I had a really arrogant attitude. I grew up with the work ethic that success is hard work."

Disruptive Intervention: "Serendipitously, I met a woman on a plane and she commented that I had a lot of Light, but I was blocked. I had no idea what she was talking about. It was a new way to see the world, and I began to see that what she was talking about made perfect sense to me because it filled the 'gap' of what I was feeling, even among all my financial success. I ended being coached by her for years and, at first, she was speaking a language I had never heard before. And, if I had, I probably made fun of it and thought it was another LA 'thing.'"

Disruptive Paradigm Shift: Meltzer confessed, "I realized that I was living by the needs of my ego, and that is when I was feeling arrogant and lost. I learned how to have less fear and doubt. When I feel the fear or doubt now, which is far less, I put Light on the fear with a big ball of Light through my third eye. The fear and doubt are now fleeting thoughts versus a destructive thought/energy that makes me stuck." He goes on to say, "I only focus in on the value of an idea or project and then maintain enthusiasm toward it. Everything already exists, and it's a matter of just waiting for its manifestation."

Results: David was able to pull out of his bankruptcy, where he'd lost everything, and also was able to maintain his marriage through this learning and conscious awareness. He feels more successful now as a whole person than ever before! And, once again, he's financially wealthy as well.

A New Visualization No One Talks About

The Universe flows at a very high energy level and frequency. When you tune in your thoughts to this level of high vibrational energy, you start to see and feel how things start to flow more easily. And, when they don't, you accept "what is" rather than resist it. You start to see you don't have to work so hard to receive the results you want. And you also realize that suffering is a choice. Suffering happens when we don't accept what is, but rather argue for what "should" be. A new visualization is one that David Meltzer implements: He uses a bright ball of light to embrace the fear, then associates the fear with something he loves and puts the bright ball of light seen through his third eye (a little higher up than between his physical eyes) over that and then the bright light over his entire body. It shifts the negative energy, and it dissolves, leaving only the "truth."

Thought Tips:

- Clear any thought that is not in harmony with Abundance.
- Are your thoughts making you move forward or stopping you in your tracks?
- Words matter *always!!*

Realignment Tip:

Compassionate Self-Forgiveness
"I lovingly forgive myself for judging myself as _____ or for _____."

What Is Your Intentional Thought?

My Intention is to let go of blaming, judgment, and criticism of myself or others.

My Intention is to think harmonizing and high-energy vibrational thoughts today.

My Intention is to be awake and be conscious of what I am feeling.

My Intention is to be ready to shift any thought or emotion that does not serve me or my business.

Successful Shifting Exercises

Moving Up Your Thought Vibrational Energy

Take out your journal and answer the following questions:

1. What am I saying to myself during the day?
2. What thoughts am I thinking about in this situation?
3. What are the emotions coming up from my thoughts now?
4. Is this the energy I want to be feeling? Or connecting to?
5. What outcome will this vibrational energy create?
6. Do I have the power to change these thoughts *now*?
7. Do I have the power to make a transformative shift *right now*?
8. Am I willing, right now, to connect with a higher-energy vibration?

Connecting with This Powerful Source

You're probably wondering how you can connect to this powerful energy source. In fact, this energy source is always available to you any second of the day to plug into. Some of the ways you can plug in, at any moment, to connect with the Universal flow of high-energy thoughts and make significant shifts in your consciousness are:

- Think of small things that you believe to be true.
- Appreciate yourself, first and foremost, for wanting to do the right thing and make a life-serving shift for your business and for your life.
- Look around you and "see" the beauty that exists in nature.
- Thank yourself for wanting to make a difference in the world with your project or business.
- Connect inside with that place of Loving and visualize that Love going throughout your body and then extending out to everything and everyone you meet that day.
- Send Loving energy to a specific situation today that is surrounded by conflict; or send that Loving energy to yourself when you feel self-doubt or are feeling "less-than."
- Use the bright light to encircle any fear or self-doubt... or any other negative thought.

This level of Thought energy is what is required to power up Quantum Synchronicity®. This is a Universal Law that all of life lives by. You get to choose your thoughts every second of the day. It's literally up to you to decide how you want your business and life to go.

What you are thinking at any given time are the feelings that you will create at that moment. If your thoughts center around upset and blame, then you will feel angry, upset, frustrated. All your emotions, communication, and actions are fueled by your thoughts and the energy behind them.

When your thoughts (mind) and your feelings (heart) connect and harmonize into higher-vibrational energy, then your purpose and passion merge seamlessly, and a new level of abundance will flow toward the results that you desire. This is what creates higher-vibrational energy, feeling in the flow, feeling on-top-of-the-world, and allows for positive chemicals, endorphins, to circulate throughout your body.

Generation Why Not?®
Breakthrough Bonus Download #2
15 Success Affirmations
Bonus download here: www.ruthklein.com/why-not-bonuses

Meditation of a Powerful You
Listen to it here: www.ruthklein.com/why-not-bonuses

Song that captures the essence of the chapter:
"Greatest Love of All" by Whitney Houston

CHAPTER 6

QUANTUM SYNCHRONICITY® PRINCIPLE #3: THE SECRET ENERGY OF BELIEFS

"You don't become what you want, you become what you believe."
Oprah Winfrey

Our thoughts inform our beliefs, and our beliefs are tightly wrapped around our basic values. Our beliefs inform the way we live. Our beliefs drive our life. We will die for what we believe to be true, and it takes awareness, or a "wake-up" call, to change or tweak a long-held belief. We create our belief system from our nuclear family's values and upbringing, our culture, and our experiences. However, we form the majority of our beliefs very early in life. And, unless we "check them out" or update them, we may be living a very limited life.

We all see life through a different perceptual lens that is made up of what our parents, teachers, family members, and the culture said was true. And many of these beliefs are created between the ages of two and eight. We continue to live our lives in our twenties, forties, and even sixties from the perceptual lens of what we learned many decades earlier. And most people never look back to reflect or question the "truth" of these beliefs!

And, every time we have an experience that fits this belief, it gives us even more "proof" that our beliefs are true and real, no matter how limiting or hurtful they may be. The interesting thing about beliefs is that, once we decide to hold a belief within our hearts, we find things that people say and do that validate our initial beliefs. This is a good thing, until it's not. For example, let's say that a parent who is upset says to a child, more than once, that what they did was "stupid." The child only hears "My mom or dad (or whoever) thinks I'm stupid." Think about it, the parent says it out of anger or frustration, not really saying that the child is stupid, but what they did was stupid. But, with the cognitive understanding of a young child, they start to believe they are stupid!

Now, that child will most likely go through most of their life thinking they are stupid and will find "proof" for this belief in many situations as they go through life. They may hear a fourth-grade peer say something they did or said was stupid…chalk one up for validation that "I'm stupid." Most likely, in both situations, the people saying it didn't mean it literally, but a child's cognitive ability is one of taking things literally.

For example, a multimillion-dollar entrepreneur heard that there was something "wrong" with her within her family throughout her time at home. In fact, she was put in an insane asylum for a brief period because her parents saw her as being very different and thought there was something wrong with her. She ended up gaining a lot of weight (she unconsciously felt she needed to protect herself), and the food she was eating was not nutritious.

As it turns out, when I worked with her, I realized she was an "Indigo Child." When I asked her if she was, she immediately started to cry. She didn't really consciously know what it was, but she connected to the word/concept intuitively! An Indigo Child is said to have special, unusual intuitive abilities and is very sensitive and wise beyond their years.

It is challenging and complex to really "see" our own belief system. What may seem like coincidences are actually energetic Synchronicity—connecting your energy vibration with that of the Universe's energy vibration. And we attract the energy vibration that we give out into the world, no matter what it is we *say* we want. And what we give out is reflected back to us, positive or not.

For example, one of my clients is a very smart and attractive entrepreneur. Her younger brother was told he was smart, and she was told she was pretty but not smart. So, through the perceptual lens of her family, winning several beauty pageants, and others telling her how pretty she was, she received "proof" and validated that she was pretty but not smart. That was her interpretation. Being smart was somehow in the domain of only her younger brother. She now says that her heart was never in the beauty pageants or in the glamour field. She felt that it was what was expected of her and she was good at it. And those same beliefs of being pretty but not smart carried over with her in relationships, where the men she dated were controlling and she would forget who she was and what she wanted. She said she was easily swayed to follow their way of thinking.

Here's the good news: By going through a process of updating her beliefs to what is real for her today—and, actually, has been for decades—she now feels in alignment with who she is, and most recently, she has fallen in love with a man who is generous, allows her to be herself, is encouraging, and sees her intelligence. She was able to attract a different type of man into her life because she saw herself differently. The energy of her newfound belief in herself was being reflected back to her with this new man. In other words, her boyfriend mirrors to her who she sees in the mirror now. Someone resourceful, smart, kind, attractive, and focused on her new career.

That is the most profound thing about beliefs. Your outer experiences reflect your internal Intentions, Thoughts, Beliefs. And your decisions are based on your beliefs. Through my studies at the University of Santa Monica (USM), Dr. Mary Hulnick, executive vice president of USM, and Dr. Ron Hulnick, president of USM, would often say, based on two Spiritual Psychology Principles: "Outer experience is a reflection of inner reality," and "Personal internal reality is subjective. Therefore, what you believe determines your experience."

Another very helpful Spiritual Psychology insight is: "How you go through the issue *is* the issue." In other words, your Thoughts, Beliefs, and Actions during a disturbance are really the issue…not necessarily the actual disturbance or circumstances of what just happened. Leigh Steinberg, the real "Jerry Maguire" that Tom Cruise portrayed in the 1996 movie, experienced divorce and health issues with his two sons. He says, "I struggled with alcohol in the wake of personal reversals; death of my father, two homes with mold infestation, two boys had an eye disease that ultimately got them to be blind and a divorce." His method of relaxation and dealing with these issues was to drink excessively to numb his feelings. In other words, how he was going through the issue is the issue. The issue wasn't his outside circumstances; it was how he was going through it. So the issue was his heavy drinking, denial, and alcohol addiction. And it was the issue of *how* he handled all the events he was experiencing that fueled his divorce and the end of his sports agent company at the time.

Leigh has been sober for years now and he envisioned a world that doesn't exist presently. He said, "I imagined everything I love to do in life and create a career around it." He's written two *New York Times* bestselling books and has created a new successful business and life. The way he handled this new part of his life is the issue…positive, new beginning, "I can" attitude, and letting go of what no longer served him.

In fact, Leigh has since recreated a top sports agency, and been named Man of the Year over a dozen times by a variety of groups including the March of Dimes, the Orange County, and Los Angeles divisions of the Anti-Defamation League, and several other professional and charitable organizations. Today he continues his unwavering commitment to make a positive impact on the world.

Paradoxical Beliefs

Life has a way of mirroring back to us our Thoughts and Beliefs. There's an interesting phenomenon called Paradoxical Beliefs. These are beliefs that run counter to what we say we want. The competing beliefs come from our subconscious, and our updated beliefs come from our consciousness. The key is to transfer the new, conscious, updated beliefs to the subconscious—the part that drives our actions, even though we say we want things to be different. This is the primary reason it's difficult to stick to New Year's resolutions or go on a diet. Unless you uncover the deeper issue that is running the show called your life, your good Intentions most likely end up on deaf ears. Paradoxical Beliefs show up often around money. Here's an example: Susan, a client who was an attorney, was always wanting to make more money. She said, no matter what she did, she basically made the same amount of money, year after year.

In order to find out what was going on with her at a deeper level, I asked her a few questions:

1. What did you hear about money growing up?
2. When you think of "money," what are other words you could replace it with?

Answers:

1. "Money doesn't grow on trees"; "You have to work hard to make anything in life"; "Don't waste money on luxu-

ries"; "We don't have enough money"; "Everything is too expensive."

2. Security, not enough, hard, luxury, save.

Even though Susan was an excellent and smart attorney, she had competing beliefs around money. On the conscious level, she wanted to make more, and, certainly, as an attorney, she felt she "should" be able to make that happen.

On the subconscious level, the competing and more dominant belief was it has to be hard to make money, she would not be able to buy luxuries, she would never have enough money. And that is exactly what showed up in her life for decades.

Once Susan was, with coaching, able to uncover the competing beliefs she had held for decades, she opened up to a new and more truthful belief around money and was able to let go of the old limiting belief.

Within two years, Susan has tripled her income!

Open to Possibilities

Once we are open to what could be…open to possibilities outside of what we believe is possible…amazing things begin to happen.

The late Steve Jobs, CEO of Apple, wanted his design team to put a specific plan together, and rumor has it that they said it couldn't be done. He then said, "Do it anyway." And you know what? They found a way because they stayed open to "Why Not? Let's keep trying and see what happens." The rest is history, as they say. The old adage, once again, is powerful: "Where there is a will, there is a way."

I have found that, the moment I say "no" and close my mind to other options, the idea dies and my belief is, "I can't do it." Over the years, I've learned to say, "How can I make this work?"

Here's an example where I started to ask myself, "How can I make this work?" I wanted to drive from my home to a business meeting in Los Angeles but would be in the height of rush hour traffic once I got to LA, which was two hours away. Years earlier, I had made a decision to eliminate business meetings at night, so I could be with my family. So how was I going to make it to the meeting in LA during rush hour and not leave my family?

Here was my download: Have my then-husband leave work a little earlier, round up the three children, and pack up their pajamas. Then, we'd be together in the car for a few hours driving there. Then, the family would drop me off at my meeting for a few hours while their dad took them out to dinner and a round of miniature golf. Then, they would get into their nighties before picking me up. And that's exactly what happened. The extra bonus was, when they picked me up after my meeting, the children were so excited to tell me about their evening and then, one by one, they fell asleep in the car coming home.

Did I care they didn't brush their teeth that one night? No.

Did I care that the children got to bed late that night? No.

I knew it was a winner when one of the children asked a few weeks later, "Mom, when do you have that meeting in LA again?"

What I loved about this scenario was that everyone was taken care of in a way that allowed them to be connected to family and have fun! Why was that so important to me? Because one of my core beliefs is being conscious of deep and meaningful connections with family, friends, clients, and myself!!

So why is it, then, that so many people coming from so many different backgrounds and ages are able to triumph and keep moving forward to achieve their vision…their dreams…their purpose…even in the face of self-doubt and/or traumatic events?

Through my interviews, experiences, and research, Generation Why Not?® finds their beliefs to be their greatest source of motivation, rather than their greatest source of limitation. However, in most cases, that wasn't always the case. They learned, some through traumatic events or trial and error, some through meditation, others through mentors and education. In all cases, they experienced a pivotal moment where they changed and transformed their limiting beliefs to empowering ones where they saw a clearer path to reaching their dreams; one in which their Intentions, Thoughts, Beliefs, and Actions started to come into alignment.

Life has a beautiful way of letting us know that our internal belief system may be off balance. It lets us know that whenever we feel upset. Whenever we feel that someone "should" have said or done something differently than what they did; or we blame the other person for feeling hurt; or we get angry "because" of what someone did, then we immediately know that our beliefs can be updated.

The most exquisite part to all this is that you have the perfect internal guidance that, when activated and called upon, opens you up to a whole new perceptual filter of possibility. This internal guidance system is the deepest level of your authentic self and, many times, will run counter to your ego. Our egos have good intentions, and there was a time when certain beliefs were useful. One of the best ways to know if a belief is still useful is if it brings negative emotions or a feeling of joy.

Your authentic self is always the positive "voice" that opens you up to new ideas, creativity, and going beyond your limiting ego-based fears. So, when you're ready to give a presentation and you only feel fear and dread, that's usually a good sign that your ego is in control.

Here are the internal beliefs that stopped me from speaking for several years: "I'm not going to speak anymore…it makes me so nervous, anyway." "I don't know why I said 'yes' to giving the speech. I don't even like to speak." After every speech I wouldn't know if my speech went well unless I read the evaluations. And, even then, if I scored 97 percent as an excellent speaker, I would focus on the comments of the other 3 percent. I did this for years, and it was exhausting!

Since the Universe brings us exactly what we need to know to keep learning and growing, I was talking to a group of people about a subject, and one of the women present said, "Well, you speak so well because you're a public speaker, Ruth." I took it as an underhanded compliment. However, that is what it took for me to "see" that I saw myself very differently than others perceived my speaking. It caused me to look closely at the beliefs I had around giving speeches. Interestingly enough, the belief of being judged when I was much younger came into full expression in this scenario! Another example of our beliefs starting when we're young!

What I realized in the process of journaling is that I was afraid of being judged. My speaking was dependent on how others evaluated "me." I took the evaluations personally and felt judged at each speech…during the whole speech, I believe I was concerned about being judged by the audience: "Am I making an impact? Am I losing their interest?" Through that exercise, I realized I was completely other-directed, and my ego was limiting me from feeling free and authentic as a speaker. What others thought of me was more important than anything else…whoa!!!

Having transformed my old limiting belief into a new life-serving belief, it sounds like this:

"There's a reason I've been asked to speak, and whoever shows up, be it three or three hundred people, they are here to hear what I have to say; because if I can make an impact that helps any of them to transform, download a new insight, or motivate them to think or do something they haven't done before, then my speech is a success!"

As a result, I love giving speeches today, although I still do get a bit nervous right before I go on. My belief around speaking that was initially governed by my ego (feeling judged) was transformed by my authentic self, where I was able to see clearly without fear or limitation. I was able to transform the negative energy based on fear to expansion and positive energy that was motivating rather than limiting me.

So let's look at some of the limiting beliefs that have, until now, been thwarting your dreams and desires to have more enjoyable and successful businesses, relationships, finances, health, and time.

The Biology of Beliefs

Dr. Bruce Lipton, the author of *The Biology of Belief*, says: "We are the ones who can change the environment or change our perception of the environment and, in that case, we have control above the genes—we have epigenetics. Here is the profound difference: we go from a belief that our health is the consequence of being a victim of our mechanical biology to realizing that our health is predominantly under the control of our perception and our environment. This becomes a change from *victim* to *master*—and this is why it is so important."

What Happens When You Get Attached to Your Story That No Longer Serves You?

Your thoughts are where your story begins. It's up to you to change the story if it's not working for you in business or any part of your life. Your thoughts give way to feelings, and the intensity of those feelings impacts our beliefs. And the first place to start to change your story is with your thoughts. Let me share a few stories created by the thoughts in these business owners.

Millennials, Generation X-ers, and Baby Boomers have created different stories, to a large degree, based on the external experiences they've had growing up. As a result, the stories that dominate among the Millennials are that they want a career that makes a difference, and they want to know how they make a difference.

Millennials were brought up during a turbulent and heavy recession and high divorce rate. They don't trust authority and would rather spend their money on experiences with friends than make big purchases. Their buying power is also restricted because of the high student debt owed.

Generation X is more of a silent generation, although they are among the most highly educated with 35 percent with college degrees. A whopping 55 percent of startup founders are in Generation X, according to an article in *Forbes* magazine.

Boomers were brought up in calm times until they hit the turmoil of the Vietnam War and they realized the need for activism, as heard in songs by musicians such as Joan Baez; Bob Dylan; and Peter, Paul, and Mary.

Molly was excellent with numbers and became an accountant. Even though she didn't enjoy it much, her thoughts kept her "stuck" counting others' numbers, as she likes to say. Then, one day, she realized that the only thing keeping her tied to her accounting practice was her thoughts!! The thought pattern of fear came across loudly. She started with the "What if" questions. She was living in her mind, and she couldn't move forward because her thoughts were becoming obsessive. And they continued to go around and around with the same anxiety due to her "futurizing" until, one day, she decided to take action and break the cycle of "just thinking" obsessive thoughts and let go of her old story. She asked herself, "Why couldn't I become an international speaker?" Three years later, she is speaking internationally as a transformational speaker.

Sharon's story was centered around the difficulty of dividing her nonprofit role with her own private consulting and speaking business attached to her nonprofit, and she couldn't see herself as the creative brains and worthy of her value. Her limiting thoughts and beliefs cost her over a million dollars of financial freedom within the last decade.

Judgment Is the Wizard of Oz

Judgment somehow has the distinguished place as the wizard to understanding our own and others' Thoughts, Beliefs, Decisions, and Actions. Dorothy and her team thought that, if they could only get to the Almighty Wizard of Oz, then all their problems would go away, yet when they finally reached their destination, they found that the Wizard was a hoax! Well, I see judgment being the same as the Wizard of Oz…we set our judgments about ourselves and others and really believe them. And the worst part is we act accordingly with those Wizard-of-Oz beliefs toward ourselves and others. This is not the way to nurture healthy beliefs that serve you. Judgment will only cause more upset and imbalance. These judgments are "hard fought," and these internal wars are what cause emotional suffering. Let's look at some of the limiting beliefs of judgment more closely.

The Limiting Effects of Judging Yourself "Not Good Enough"

The average perceptual lens around belief consists, for most people, of fear, judgment, blame, and anxiety. I'd like to invite you to take a journey with me on how beliefs impact our lives—professionally, in relationships, with money, with time, and in our health. The limiting effects of judging yourself as "not good enough" can include:

Business: Very difficult to work with, as they are very sensitive to most feedback of any kind. Easily annoyed and ready to "protect" their integrity.

Relationships: High level of jealousy and fearful the people they love most will leave them. Many times, it becomes a self-fulfilling prophecy.

Money: Rarely make a lot of money because they don't believe they're worthy, deserving, or good enough. Spend a lot of time and money on going to conferences because they never quite feel they know enough. This "not enough" shows up in most parts of their lives.

Time: Always running short on time and likely to be late more often than early.

Health: Live with a lot of constant fear and constantly comparing themselves to others, which increases their anxiety and lowers their self-worth.

Jonathan, CEO of his company, often receives national recognition for his work, as well as for being the author of two traditionally published books that received large advances. In addition, he has been asked to speak at high-profile conferences. People and his clients rave about his programs. And yet he just couldn't attract the income he desired and knew he should be bringing in. After working with him for about six months, he was able to see that he had created a huge block in his subconscious that he wasn't good enough. He was feeling the pangs of self-doubt in almost all the decisions he needed to make and, as a result, never felt like the CEO of his company. He felt and acted more like an employee without direction from a CEO. His self-doubt merged into unhealthy time and money boundaries. He went overtime coaching his clients and charged different amounts based on what he *thought* others could pay. How did this affect his confidence, time, and finances?

- Old limiting belief—he didn't feel good enough and overdelivered to his clients to make them like him.
- Time boundaries—he often gave double the time coaching sessions.
- Money boundaries—because he didn't feel confident in his value, he would often undercharge his clients.
- Result—Jonathan felt like he was always working and didn't have much to show for it!

The Limiting Belief Effect of "Who Do You Think You Are?"

Business: A great deal of self-doubt and, as a result, it's difficult to hear constructive criticism.

Relationships: Tend to blame others for their internal sensitivities. Very often feel that people don't listen to them and feel upset and anxious as a result.

Money: The self-absorption and concern about what others think waste hours of time daily. Time that could be spent doing projects that bring in money. Very difficult for them to make a lot of money because they often feel like an "imposter."

Time: They may spend an inordinate amount of time trying to "show" others their self-worth and how "smart" they are, but beneath all that "show" is someone who is spending a great deal of time worrying, which disrupts focus and completion of tasks.

Health: Suffer from a lot of stress and anger almost every day. This stress and anger affect internal organs, such as the brain and liver, and hormone levels of cortisol go through the roof. Many people end up suffering from adrenal fatigue.

The Limiting Belief Effect of Perfectionism

Business: There never seems to be enough time to get the work done "properly."

Relationships: Increased stress hanging over them because they're constantly caught between not having enough time to get a project done and worrying that it isn't ready…or perfect.

Money: Works three times harder than necessary and is almost always running on extra energy. Because of the extra time consumed, they have less money to show for it and can't understand why.

Time: Never enough time, so they spend two to three times longer on a project. Always trying to beat the clock and "running out of time."

Health: Feel burnout frequently and that they need a vacation, but are too busy to take one.

Jenny, the CEO of her company, wanted to start a new division in her business. She continued to make outlines of what she wanted to do, but nothing went beyond the planning stages. She loved to spend time planning and then doing more planning. She was caught in a cycle of perfectionism—always trying to "perfect" something. She didn't want to make a mistake because it weighed heavily on her that her service programs would not be received well from her clients, so she spent nearly two years trying to develop just the right service program for her clients. Her perfectionism was tied directly to the way she thought of herself…as lesser than, not good enough, not smart enough, not pretty enough…all of what I call the "not enough thinking." And, when she looked in her inbox and saw what others were doing, she found herself comparing herself to what others were doing, and that only dug a deeper hole into her self-confidence, thus perpetuating the always-planning stage—another name for perfectionism.

Generation Why Not?® Alert! Generation Why Not?® tends to be a group driven to succeed, no matter what. Although that may seem quite admirable at first glance, the downside is they may end up working long hours at the expense of health and relationships.

Three Belief Patterns of Attachment

Attachment is a common bedfellow in business and life. It shows up when we are unable to see or accept "what is," but rather we are attached to the behavior, person, or outcome and get upset when the results don't look like what we had imagined. Let's look at each one of these a little closer and how each can show up in our lives and can limit us to reaching our true potential.

1. **Misidentification**—Misidentification takes place when we identify with being someone or something that we are not. For example, in my own life, I remember very vividly all the times I would be asked to go "play" during the middle of the workday and I would almost always say, "No, I have the Immigrant's Work Ethic." I identified myself with a label that was not who I was, but rather a thought I had that was created years earlier while watching my parents work seven days a week and rarely even taking a day off…for decades! The same type of misidentification happens when someone says they're an alcoholic or an addict, lawyer, doctor, or that they are smart or whatever. The truth is that you are a Divine Being having human experiences. In other words, you are not your experiences. You are a loving and kind Spirit. And Quantum Synchronicity®: The Method helps guide you to remembering who you truly are underneath all the external circumstances, misinterpretations, and misidentifications you may be holding as deep beliefs that cause you upset, grief, and anxiety.

2. **Attached to the Person (an example of a business partner…or any type of partner, actually)**—This type of attachment can limit your potential and the value and worth you bring to your professional life. This happens, particularly, when there are partnerships. If one partner ends the relationship, one or both of the people involved lose their direction; they feel abandoned, used,

hurt, a failure…you name your dagger, and those are the thoughts that lead your life for a while. When the person leaves or gets sick, the other partner, many times, feels that they can't do what is necessary because they have learned to attach themselves and their success to the other person. This is particularly seen in love relationships when a partner dies or through a divorce. The surviving spouse doesn't remember who they are; they don't think they know how to keep going on, and other attachments with the spouse who "left."

3. **Attached to the Outcome/Results**—This is where I find most CEOs and entrepreneurs. They get attached to the outcome…the results they think they "should" produce. When you hear yourself saying the "should" word, you may want to remember that living with "should" will only limit your progress because you get "stuck" or attached to how you think it "should" go, closing the door to the power of other options and possibility. The main limitation here is that, as a result, four things often happen:

   1) The CEO thinks they are a failure or the project is a failure and is at a loss to move forward; or 2) They are so focused on getting their predetermined results that anything less than that doesn't count; or 3) They are so focused on what they want that they are not open to other options; or 4) The financial health of the business is at stake.

Beliefs matter!

Generation Why Not?®
Breakthrough Bonus Download #3
How to Rewrite Your Story Success Template
Bonus download here: www.ruthklein.com/why-not-bonuses

Meditation on Letting Go of Upset with Gratitude
Listen to it here: www.ruthklein.com/why-not-bonuses

Song that captures the essence of the chapter:
"Brave" by Sara Bareilles

CHAPTER 7

QUANTUM SYNCHRONICITY® PRINCIPLE #4: THE SECRET ENERGY OF DECISION

"Trust that your soul has a plan, and even if you can't see it completely, know that everything will unfold as it is meant to."
Deepak Chopra

What's so beautiful during the process of making decisions is that we make them almost every minute of the day. You decide when you're going to get up and out of bed; what to wear, eat, and listen to; which path to take to work; and tens of thousands more choices each day.

And, since we live in a sea of decisions all day long, how do we keep moving forward and motivated, rather than just automatically doing what we've always done…in the same way and manner, stuck in a rut?

I invite you to open up to the possibility to think in a new way…a new paradigm for making conscious decisions. In fact, research tells us that we make 226.7 decisions daily on food alone; 35,000 decisions a day, mostly not conscious, but based on habit. And here's the good news: old habits can be changed into fresh practices that will make your life one that you create, versus living by force of habit, routine, or default.

Generation Why Notter Joe Swinger, author of *Awaken the Magic Within…The 7 Essential Virtues for Incredible Success*, used to be considered the "manager from hell."

"There was a time when I was a sales manager for a large corporation," Joe says, "and gave a lot of critical and judgmental feedback to the people that I managed, but never could I accept any feedback from them. When someone gave me feedback, I immediately went to a place inside and felt lesser than and judged. It was all because of how I was brought up and the beliefs I had about myself. It came down to me having very low self-esteem. And all my decisions were coming from a place of lack…of feeling lesser than and seeing myself as not valuable as an employee or even as a person. It's taken many years of personal and business development to make changes in some deep-seated beliefs about myself. Today, I'm considered a great coach and mentor by my team and my private clients and everything I do now comes from a place of being in service to others—always looking at ways to help them."

Joe says, "I had to journey to the depths of losing everything so that I could find the leader within. I see that the story was an illusion that I bought completely and believed in." After personal and business development, Joe was able to embrace active listening, awareness, commitment to growth, stewardship, and community building within his teams, and the results were amazing: he raised profits by 30 percent, empowered his team and accepted their ideas, and was open to listening to new possibilities to increase sales.

The New Paradigm for Making Decisions

Generation Why Not?® looks at making decisions differently than most people. They focus on making decisions that fit with their major values. It is not a decision made based on what another will like or how it will please others, but a determination arrived at because it is in full alignment with what they find to be important and valuable.

In his interview with me, Generation Why Notter Nick Taranto said that the many decisions he makes for his company are difficult, but he is guided by the information at hand, his experiences, and Intuition. And he trusts that his decision is the best decision at that time. Trusting yourself to reach the right decision based on information, facts, experiences, and Intuition are the major parameters that members of Generation Why Not?® are guided by.

Nothing is by accident, and learning to take the leadership role in making decisions is a perfect way to grow in trust, patience, and kindness as a human being and as a leader.

The Decision to Take 100 Percent Responsibility

Generation Why Not?® takes 100 percent responsibility for their words, thoughts, decisions, actions, and life. We experienced "defining moments" as we were growing up. And we made a decision during those "pivotal moments" because we interpreted things that people said or did…or because of the external circumstances we found ourselves in, leading to how we interpreted those words, actions, circumstances. And it is those pivotal decisions that start to define the quality and type of life we live… based on our interpretation or, more specifically, misinterpretation. This isn't good or bad…it just is. Developmental psychologists have suggested that cognitive reasoning usually comes into being at the age of six. And, if we made pivotal decisions from the age of three to nine, for example, then we are still living out the decisions we made in grade school well into our twenties, thirties, forties, fifties, sixties, and even seventies…unless we take the time to consciously pay attention to the life we've created and become aware of our beliefs and decisions based on those beliefs. Joe Swinger is a perfect example of this, as he grew up in a family where he felt not good enough. That pivotal decision he made as a young boy stayed with him throughout most of his adult life and as a result, he had difficulties at work, home, and personally. In fact, he found himself homeless. It was that experience that motivated him to start transforming his life into the life he wanted. He's now an author and a midlife transformational coach, and lives a joyful life with his wife of several decades.

Sam, a corporate leadership trainer, had difficulty building a relationship with his team. He also decided that "when you love someone, they'll leave you" after his father abandoned the family when he was seven years old. This anxiety manifested itself in his business team, with client communications, and in his personal relationships. He was unable to stay in a romantic relationship for over six months because: "I knew she would eventually leave me, so I needed to get out before I would have that heartbreak." And his fear became a self-fulfilling prophecy! Why? Because he made a pivotal decision using the cognitive ability of a seven-year-old, thirty-two years earlier!

What happened? Sam made an association between building a relationship of any kind with loving and leaving. He said, "I have always felt that I didn't belong because I felt others rejected me." Our work together was to have him "see" that his subconscious was leading his life and how being open to a new paradigm lens of reality today would shift his Thoughts, Beliefs, and Decisions he made. He was finally able to change careers, and he went into business for himself. What kept him from doing that earlier? Sam's fear of being rejected in sales. However, once he became aware of this driving belief in his life, he was able to update and choose a more truthful belief. He made the commitment to change and create the business and life he always wanted. As of this writing, Sam has been in a romantic relationship for over eighteen months.

Here is a beautiful quote from British mountaineer William Hutchison Murray's 1951 book, *The Scottish Himalayan Expedition*, that I've always felt recognizes the power of Energy combined with Synchronicity:

"Until one is committed, there is hesitancy,
the chance to draw back, always ineffectiveness.
Concerning all acts of initiative (and creation), there is
one elementary truth, the ignorance of which kills countless
ideas and splendid plans: that the moment one definitely
commits oneself, then Providence moves too. All sorts
of things occur to help one that would never otherwise
have occurred. A whole stream of events issues from the
decision, raising in one's favour all manner of unforeseen
incidents and meetings and material assistance, which
no man could have dreamt would have come his way.

I have learned a deep respect for one of Goethe's couplets:

'Whatever you can do, or dream you can, begin it.
Boldness has genius, power, and magic in it!'"

The World of Choice

In *Think and Grow Rich Every Day*, self-help author Napoleon Hill wrote:

"The man of DECISION cannot be stopped.
The man of INDECISION cannot be
started! Take your own choice."

Neal Katz, a twenty-five-year-old autistic young man, is definitely a Generation Why Notter, and one of the interviewees for this book. He is an emissary for autism and has made presentations twice at the United Nations; gives paid speeches nationally, even though he can't talk; had a walk-on part in the Netflix hit TV series *Atypical* and was a star of the two-time Emmy award-winning 2008 HBO documentary *Autism: The Musical*, featuring The Miracle Project created by Hollywood acting and international autism speaker and coach, Elaine Hall. Neal can now use an electronic communication device to share his thoughts and, in his PowerPoint presentation, *Living a Meaningful Life: Motormorphosis*, he asserts: "I want my reader to know that even people with severe disabilities, autism in my case, know how important decisions are to their lives and the power of choice." Neal goes on to say, "Choice is what defines a real life."

And you have the choice to make different decisions about how you're thinking, believing, and feeling. But first, let's look at the distinction between making decisions governed by Ego or Spirit/Intuition. Decisions based on Ego are fear-based, while decisions based on Spirit are abundance and acceptance based.

Is It Ego or Spirit Speaking?

So many of my clients ask me, "How do I know if it's Ego or Intuition guiding me?" I have to say this is an excellent question and all the more reason to be present and mindful when we "hear" that small voice talking inside of us. It's usually the voice of wisdom. If that little voice sounds punishing or critical, you know that little voice comes from fear...from the Ego. Let's look at some examples that will help you to decide for yourself.

If the "voice" inside is anywhere near blaming, shaming, or judging you, then you immediately know it is coming from Fear and is not Spirit. If you or someone you know says, "I'm upset because…" this is a dead giveaway that they are coming from fear and Ego. They are not coming from a place where they take 100 percent responsibility for being upset, no matter what the circumstances are. I know that is difficult to hear and even believe. But, when you start to look at the situation or the action that just happened, you have the opportunity to ask yourself, "What part did I play in this?" or "What part of me is being triggered right now?"

If the voice you hear is Loving and you just have a sense of "knowing," then it is most likely Spirit. Spirit protects you with Love, not shame or blame! Decisions based on Spirit and Abundance do not recognize fear, worry, and anxiety, because It is "all-knowing" and realizes that things are working for the Greater Good and within a larger plan, so there's no need for anxiety or worry!

Here are some things to consider when making decisions and trying to figure out if they are driven by fear or "Truth":

Perfectionism: One of the voices that many people "hear" comes from a need to "be" or "do" perfectly. It is their way to feel "good enough" and "smart enough." You can see that not feeling good enough comes from shame or judging yourself as not being good enough. I have found that shame, blame, and judgment, whether toward yourself or toward others, only short-circuits the Intuitive connection and leaves you feeling negatively or badly toward yourself or others. In the world of

Quantum Synchronicity®, negativity attracts the very things you don't want because shame, blame, and judgment are very low vibrational energies, no matter what!

The Need to Be Right: Somewhere along the way, we believe we need to make sure that, when people speak, they are accurate and say things that are correct...or we need to "clue" them in. This type of communication gets really painful in relationships. And all of us are in relationships—work, family, clients, vendors, friends, yourself. Everyone's "right" is very much based on their values and beliefs. So focus on being right for yourself and in alignment with your values.

The Need to Feel Offended: Bestselling author and Generation Why Notter David Meltzer is a big believer that it's necessary to let go of the need to feel offended. When you are not invited to something; when someone says something that is not kind toward you; when the family dynamics don't include you...whatever it is that "offends" you, it's time to let it go, and that little voice is working big time in Ego. I don't want to give our Egos a bad rap...they have their purpose, just like everything else. Our life-serving Ego is where we feel confident, want to start a family, get married or stay single, not have children, or change careers for a bigger salary.

The Ego is life-draining when it starts to feel it needs to "protect" us and does this by offering us things to be fearful about, worry over, and judge ourselves or others in order to feel "safe" or "good."

Judgment: This is something that runs rampant and has for centuries. We worry about what others will think of us. This is where we end up in professions and careers "for others," rather than really wanting it ourselves. This is where we end up with bigger and better, not because we truly want it, but because we think that bigger is truly better, as this is what we've learned to expect in our culture. Nowhere is this more widely accepted than in the restaurant business. People will tend to pay more when they get more food. Perhaps they're looking at quantity rather than quality. Whenever you hear the little voice that is connected with feeling "less than," you most likely know it's Ego speaking!

In addition, if you can understand the person or situation, it will deactivate judgment. That is one of the primary reasons that relationships of all types work, for the most part, when you can understand the other person and offer them compassion as a human being. The same applies to you as well. This is where many people get off balance and critically self-judge themselves. When you offer yourself understanding and compassion for being human and doing the best you can at the time, you help deactivate self-judgment.

Seven Patterns of Decision-Makers

I have found seven primary decision-making patterns. I invite you to identify your dominant decision-making style. Then, think of the last decision you made and what the emotional motivation was behind it.

Let's look at the seven styles now and the emotional motivation that may be lurking behind them. The seven styles are:

Analyzers—This is when there never seems to be enough information to make a decision.

> *Emotional Motivator:* Fear of being wrong, and not trusting the information they've uncovered so far, or their experiences and Intuition.
>
> *Time and Money Impact:* There's never enough.
>
> *Positive Affirmation to Move Forward:* "I will review seven things and make my decision from there. Seven is not statistically significant, but it does show a trend. I feel confident that, whatever I find, I will trust the info I've gathered, use my other experiences and Intuition, and go forward with a decision."

Perfectionists—They can wait, and, while it looks like procrastination, it's really that the person doesn't want to make a mistake….

They're usually very closely connected to their self-worth.

> *Emotional Motivator:* Usually, there's a need to be perfect due to a deep belief of not being good enough.
>
> *Time and Money Impact:* There isn't enough because of the time and money they spend to have something be "perfect" and they are still not pleased with the outcome.
>
> *Positive Affirmation to Move Forward:* "I know there isn't perfection in anything, including me. I also know that I am enough, just the way I am…now! I accept myself for who I am."

Risk-takers—All life is a risk, at some level. My uncle broke his hip in his own home when he was eighty-nine years old. We never know what is on the other side of any given moment. Taking risks is a normal part of life and business. Within the minds of Generation Why Notters is an excitement and a passion to go for it…to try and see what happens.

> *Emotional Motivator*: Excitement to create something new. Coming from a place of more abundance. Why Not? Once I decide I'm going to go for it, I'm going with complete focus and passion!
>
> *Time and Money Impact:* They're able to leverage time and money by staying very focused on keeping healthy time and money boundaries.
>
> *Positive Affirmation to Move Forward:* "I have done my homework, and I'm ready to go. I will only know what is the best direction for me once I take action and just start…now! I'm going to make a commitment and take action and allow the Universe to help support me along the way, in ways I could never even imagine. I can do this!"

Fence-sitters—It is difficult to prioritize what's most important in a situation in order to make a good decision, so they keep waffling back and forth.

> *Emotional Motivator:* They feel stuck and paralyzed and are therefore unable to move either way out of fear that they

will make someone upset with them. They are closely attached to the outcome and/or the person.

Time and Money Impact: Opportunities come and go without much action undertaken to utilize the gifts of possibility.

Positive Affirmation to Move Forward: I see many pros and cons for each decision. If I didn't care what others think or would say, what decision would I choose?

"I Don't Know"—Undecided people go back and forth with making decisions, as they don't want to be wrong…again.

Emotional Motivator: They're confused as to what they really want, and it's easier to just say, "I don't know." This is not taking 100 percent responsibility for their decisions.

Time and Money Impact: Time escapes them easily, and they wonder where all the hours went…and, similarly, where all the money went.

Positive Affirmation to Move Forward: I always ask myself, "If I did know, what would that be?" I know my inner wisdom will give me an answer and that the first answer that comes to mind is usually the best answer.

Procrastinators—FedEx was invented for this type of decision-maker. And I'm thrilled they did for all the times I procrastinated and needed to "rush" to make a deadline!

Emotional Motivator: Don't know where to start, how to start, feel overwhelmed. They fear asking for clarity or direction out of concern that others may think they don't know what they're doing.

Time and Money Impact: Always feel they're running behind in time and in their finances.

Positive Affirmation to Move Forward: "I know the best and fastest way to pull out of feeling overwhelmed is to identify one thing I can do now and do it! The first action will build momentum, and I can keep going from there. I will also take advantage of small time spans, such as when I have five minutes, ten minutes, or fifteen minutes to take one small action to get the momentum going and bring clarity to the project at hand.

Blamers (traumatizers)—If I make this decision, then they'll be upset; they are "forcing me to make this decision, even though I don't want to." It sounds like, "I'm upset because…." And then they go on to blame or shame someone for some circumstance for why they're upset.

Emotional Motivator: Fear of being blamed, judged, or shamed themselves. They tend to project those fears— the very ones they may be feeling—onto others….

Time and Money Impact: Don't understand why time is passing them by so quickly and or why they can't seem to hold on to money.

Positive Affirmation to Move Forward: I empower myself by figuring out what I can do, say, or act differently, so I can be free of others' actions and outside circumstances. And, when I do get upset, I know it's because I'm triggered by an old thought or belief deeply embedded in my subconscious that I am sensitive to.

Any habit can be changed. That's the beauty of recognizing how your beliefs directly impact your decisions. And, as you update your beliefs, your decisions will reflect those values and be more in sync with your true essence. Your true essence is the place inside your inner self that most people would love for others to be able to see. But here's the challenge: if you don't see and appreciate your true essence, then others won't see or appreciate it either. I hear so many people in business and in love relationships saying, "I wish they really knew me, but they don't see who I am." Or "Nobody understands me." When they say this, I would immediately ask, "Do you understand you?"

The spirit of others not only influences our thoughts, moods, and sense of well-being, it shapes our decisions as well. What if you and the person you're communicating with—in any situation—came from a place of heart-centered listening and looked for the true loving essence in each other, while taking 100 percent responsibility for your Intentions, Thoughts, Words, Beliefs, Decisions, and Actions? "What type of business culture would that create and how would that affect people's motivation and productivity?" I'd say, and I have trained businesses where it increases dramatically.

At the end of the day, Why Not?

Generation Why Not?®
Breakthrough Bonus Download #4
A Decision-Making Template
Bonus download here: www.ruthklein.com/why-not-bonuses

Meditation on Easy and Confident Decision Making
Listen to it here: www.ruthklein.com/why-not-bonuses

Song that captures the essence of the chapter:
"I Hope You Dance" by Lee Ann Womack

CHAPTER 8

QUANTUM SYNCHRONICITY® PRINCIPLE #5: THE SECRET ENERGY OF ACTION

"Whatever you can do, or dream you can, begin it.
Boldness has genius, power, and magic in it."
Goethe

What does the secret energy of action mean? I'm going to share with you how the invisible energy that flows through us and around us affects us in ways that we're not aware of, unless we're conscious to this energy and we respect and honor its power. As we've mentioned previously, the Laws of the Universe—and certainly the energy that drives everything—are real and these laws can't be flexed. But that's

OK if you share the belief that we're flexible to *it* versus it is flexible for us. Taking inspired action magnifies this energy.

Inspired Action

Is there really a difference between taking action and taking inspired action? Yes! This may sound simply like semantics, although I assure you, once you've experienced "inspired action," you will certainly feel the difference. You will experience a surge of energy and productivity that comes much more easily. Inspired action is about connecting and engaging in the idea… there's the added momentum, an "aha" moment, a level of passion that inspires you. The secret to taking inspired action is to do follow-up, now!

An easy way to identify and invite inspired action into your life is to move forward on the internal voice that says something like, "Call John." It also shows up when you have what I refer to as a Divinely Gifted Download, or awesome insight that was "given" to you, and you take the idea that is wrapped in energy and excitement and you go for it. You don't wait! And, if for some reason, it's not possible for you to move on it at that moment, then:

1. Write it down and 2. put it on your calendar as the next thing/task/to-do that you undertake. Act while the iron is hot. The gift is in taking action while you feel a heightened level of energy and clarity! Clarity has everything to do with keeping momentum going…when we

feel stuck, we most likely aren't clear on the next step or how it relates to anything, and momentum slows down or stops completely. Notice that I did not say you would necessarily know "how" to get started or complete the task, but only that you have a strong feeling to move on it. Once you've accepted that piece, you will know where to look, if you need help or a resource to do it.

Generation Why Notter Arsen Marsoobian—an octogenarian (eighty-four years young), author of four books in the last six years, and semiretired insurance professional—had an inspired thought to call a fellow insurance colleague to check on his hurt ankle and followed up on it immediately. Here's what happened, and what happens regularly in my life and the lives of Generation Why Not?®. Let's look at the individual parts of this "Inspired Action":

- Internally Arsen had an idea to make a call to a colleague he hadn't spoken to for a while.
- He immediately took action on the inspiration to call.
- The conversation led to the exact missing piece of information on a new insurance product that Arsen would be presenting to a very large organization on Tuesday afternoon.
- The colleague and Arsen set up an appointment to meet by phone with the executive team of the insurance company to help Arsen with more specific information for his presentation the next day for a large association.

- Arsen says, "All I did was take inspired action, and it may result in hundreds of thousands of dollars to me as well as being able to offer an incredible insurance product for a charitable foundation. This will become my pilot presentation for similar organizations."

Arsen took inspired action and allowed the Universe to add the invisible energy of Quantum Synchronicity®.

I personally receive Divinely Gifted Downloads while I'm relaxing and not stressed. My favorite place to receive inspired action is walking along the beach early in the mornings. A dear friend of mine passed, and I went to the ocean to try to make sense of it. I didn't come up with anything that made sense of her passing, but what I did download were her words that I heard so clearly in my head: "Ruthie, live the best life you can." Then, she told me that if I ever had the chance to sit it out or dance, that she hoped I chose to dance. Wow! I was in awe of what I heard from the little voice inside.

I remembered a song with those lyrics but had forgotten the name of it. So, I walked to the car, took out my phone, and googled the words I could remember, and the song "I Hope You Dance" by Lee Ann Womack played. Besides bringing tears of joy and appreciation for "Judy's words," I also had the idea of playing the song during my two-day live event as a tribute to my dear friend! And, on the last day of the event, I was inspired to read the letter I had written to Judy the day after she passed. I asked my beautiful group if they would like for me to read it to them, and they all said, "Yes." At that moment, it all came together. The name of my live event was "Uplevel Your Brand—

Uplevel Your Business," and it was all about learning to be bold, take risks, and uplevel you…your brand. Now, once you're on the path of taking inspired action, how do you stay in action mode? It's about focus!

The Power of Focus

In today's world, filled with all types of "noise" from outside sources, as well as our own internal thoughts can be draining, to say the least. And it is estimated that today's attention span is about ten seconds. And, if someone is *interested* in hearing someone speak, research says that people will listen for twenty minutes, tops! It's no wonder that TED talks started out as eighteen minutes and now many are shorter.

You can also find this online. Networks and producers are finding the webisodes of ten to fifteen minutes are capturing the attention of many online. All this is great, unless you're wanting to focus for longer periods, which is usually a requirement to get things accomplished. I believe that you can "find" an additional two hours a day! How? Let me share a few strategies with you that have worked for me and many of my clients. The secret is to focus on priorities, rather than distractions.

Place Your "Mini-Me" Away and Off

I'm calling your cell phone your "mini-me." This one strategy will give you many "bonus hours" during the day. Put your phone away and turn it off…or, at least, mute the sound. You may find this to be difficult at first, because it is estimated that we look at our phones eighty times a day on vacation and up to three hundred times a day. I would guesstimate that we look at our phones during workdays just as much or more! Even if you figure each of those "looks" takes sixty seconds, you have to add on an additional five minutes, at least, to get back into focusing on your task at hand. So, doing the math, that equates to eighty times five minutes each, for a whopping six and a half hours…a day!! Let's make that eighty times a day for only three minutes to refocus—that equates to three hours a day.

So consider, for a moment, what would your energy, productivity, and joy factor look like if you tried to put your "mini-me" (phone) away or on mute, for half a day and work yourself up to a full day twice a week? What would you do with an extra three to six hours a week?

I can tell you from experience that it was very difficult for me to do at first, as I had become addicted to looking at my phone… for no reason other than to see if I received a text, received a "like" or comment from Instagram, or email via phone. However, once I did it, I can tell you unequivocally that my productivity and joy factor increased tenfold!

And I can also say that it takes being very present not to fall victim to my "mini-me" during my peak productivity time.

Rule of Two

Yes, there's a lot going on during the day that requires your attention: solving problems, making decisions, and so much more. So how do you get things of importance done each day? And feel as though you've been productive?

A great strategy that I have used for decades will help you stay focused on your two highest priorities for that day. Here's how it works.

Choose two top priorities that you want to get done today— two task/projects, two emails, two calls, two articles to read, two social media platforms to review or respond to...or whatever your productive day looks like.

Choose the two priorities that, if you can only do those two things (e.g., make those two calls, respond to only those two emails), will make you feel at the end of the day that you've taken care of important items and you are productive.

Once you've done those two items in each area, you go to the next two high-priority things and so on. Think about it...let's say that you only had time to do two sets of the Rule of Two...how would you feel at the end of the day? You may immediately say, "Ruth, there's no way I can only do two sets of the Rule of Two... do you know how busy I am?" Here's a way for you to answer that inquiry yourself:

- How much did you get accomplished...really productively on high-priority things yesterday?
- How many days in a row did you feel you've been productive or accomplished important things, calls, and emails?

One of the most effective ways to stay on focus is to create a habit of daily "productivity office hours" rather than looking at the whole day to get things done via willpower. Fitness gyms depend on people's willpower every January when they have their biggest sign-ups of new members. However, when that willpower is converted into a decision and a habit is created, then you have a far better chance of meeting your dreams and goals. Welcome to the Five Focused Productivity Hours!

Five Focused Productivity Hours

Here's a daily strategy I use and have been promoting for years. I call it the Focus Five Productivity Hours I utilize workdays. You will most likely find that four to five focused hours daily will provide double to triple productivity for you. Once you've established these hours as habit and commit to sticking to it, you will feel more joy and energy from your accomplishments and completions during your day.

The Five Focused Hours also allows you to lessen distractions, such as overwhelm, low mojo, not working on something because you don't feel like it, obsessive thinking of all you have to do, anxiety about not knowing what to do next, and the list goes on.

First, I want you to determine what time of the day is your highest energy. For most people, it's the morning. For some, it's the afternoon, and, for others, it may be evening. You will want to identify your high energy time of day before you start because you want to work *with* your biorhythms, not force yourself to do so.

Let's look at biorhythms, or your body's natural twenty-four-hour cycle located in the brain, for a moment. Biorhythms are an automatic and internal mechanism of your physical, emotional, and mental clock. Jet lag is all part of our biorhythm cycles. You can actually chart your biorhythms as they start from the hour you were born.

Morning people: Choose five hours in the morning for your Five Focused Productivity Hours.

My five focused hours starts at 7 a.m. most mornings. The days that I exercise to Zumba at 10:30 a.m., my productivity hours are from 7 a.m.–10 a.m., and again from 12 noon to 2 p.m., three days a week.

Late mornings: This is when your energy taps into gear. Choose five hours, starting at 11 a.m. For those of you who get started late in the afternoon, you may think about eating a protein-rich breakfast. Otherwise, as one late-morning client said, "Just as I'm getting geared up to be productive, it's time for lunch." Here's how she dealt with that. She started her productive time at 11 a.m. to 1 p.m. She then had lunch with a potential or existing client and then, after lunch, she went back into her productivity zone from 3 p.m. to 5 p.m.

Afternoon high energy: If you feel the highest energy in the afternoons, then you may want to place your five hours from noon to around 5 p.m. These are only suggestions. Find out what works best for you.

Evenings and night owls: The best strategy here might be to have a career that allows you to start your work day at 10 or 10:30 a.m. For example, my daughter is a night owl, and her profession as a realtor works very well with her biological clock.

This is how I've divided the focused five productivity hours… feel free to tweak, modify, and make it your own.

First hour: Writing

This is anything that requires your focus, attention, and creativity, whether it be a presentation, speech, article, product, or service launch.

Second hour: Marketing

Anything that requires you communicating with your targeted audience, including social media, any advertising or promotional material necessary. This is also where you would review any sponsor or influencer opportunities.

Third hour: Business Development (acquisition and maintenance)

There are two main areas of business development for every company, big or small. The first and the most common is client/customer acquisition. The other and less implemented is client/customer maintenance. Imagine an attorney, a CPA, hairdresser, manufacturer…you name it…having them contact you via phone or email to see how you're enjoying their product/service. Personally, I'd fall out of my chair, as I would imagine most people would.

Fourth hour: Anything that requires you to have direct contact with your clients/customers/employees that helps them move forward in their business, or the behind-the-scenes work you need to do for the client/customer. Anything that impacts your clients happens during this time slot.

Fifth hour: Money (review/manage billing, profit/loss, expenditures, tracking money, investing profits).

Every business, large and small, would do well to review financials, track expenditures, track profits and where they're the most profitable. Money loves attention, and that which is focused on expands. Pay attention to finding avenues to invest profits.

You can break up these five hours (e.g., two or three hours in the morning and the other two hours at another time). The most important thing to remember is to be consistent and create the habit for consistency, focus, and productivity. You will feel far less stress and overwhelm while putting this plan into effect.

Time Consciousness

I read an essay by Marcia Bjornerud, a professor of geosciences, whose book title caught my attention: *Timefulness: How Thinking Like a Geologist Can Help Save the World*. I view "timefulness" as being conscious, present, mindful of time as we go through our day. The key to staying present during the day is that we can segment our day and stay present, rather than runaway thinking about all we have to do. We simply focus on the time segment we are working on. As in any type of mindfulness, staying present eliminates anxiety and "futurizing," which causes anxiety to begin with.

Taking this timefulness into account, let's move forward and integrate it into our day for a higher level of consistency and productivity. I heartily suggest that you plan and use a month-at-a-glance calendar, whether it's online or offline. Here are the benefits of using a month-at-a-glance calendar:

- You can plan in advance, week by week, to check how heavy your schedule is, if meetings are back to back; get familiar with your travel schedule so you can plan time before and after to re-enter and focus on your work.
- It helps to lessen surprises from day to day.

- You can plan in advance what days and times of day you want to have "quiet and focus time" in your office to get high-priority items accomplished.
- You can actually divide each day visually between mornings, early afternoon, late afternoon, and evening appointments.

For example, when I plan my schedule with my month-at-a-glance calendar, my intention is to keep Monday through Friday mornings, starting at 7, the beginning of my workday.

However, on Mondays, Wednesdays, and Fridays, I start at 7 a.m. and take off for a Zumba class from 10:30 a.m. to noon. I may only make two classes a week, but I have it blocked off, nonetheless.

And, by knowing that I have a lot of "white space" in the mornings on my calendar and that I have the highest energy in the mornings, I feel very calm because I have planned for the time to work on my high priorities. I rarely have morning meetings.

If you do have morning meetings, you may want to reconsider and have them later in the day. First of all, ask yourself why you've set the meeting in the morning. And, if most of your employees are the norm, in that they are morning people with high energy, a meeting will only curtail their productivity. Morning meetings are great for your late morning or afternoon energy employees/staff.

Segmented Time Blocks

Another way to block your day for productivity is segmenting or breaking up the day into six segments to help with focus and productivity: 1) early morning, 2) late morning, 3) early afternoon, 4) late afternoon, 5) early evening, and 6) late evening.

Imagine each day on the calendar divided into six invisible blocks.

The first segment is from wake up until 10 a.m.

Second segment from 10 a.m. to noon.

Third segment from noon to 3 p.m.

Fourth segment from 3 p.m. to 6 p.m.

Fifth segment from 6 p.m. 9 p.m.

Sixth segment from 9 p.m. until bedtime.

Just by looking at my day on the calendar, I know how much open time I have for focused work by the amount of "white space" in a segment. Since I don't plan any meetings in the mornings, the first two segments of my calendar have white space. This white space allows my brain to stay focused and mindful on the work at hand. It alleviates overwhelm just by looking at my daily "white space."

Bonus Hour

Whenever someone cancels or has to reschedule a meeting, I look at it as a "Bonus Hour." You can also have a Bonus Hour when you use the Focused Five…you may find that you only need four hours to be really productive, most days. That's great—you can use the fifth hour as a Bonus Hour. Perhaps, that is where you might take twenty minutes to meditate, another twenty minutes to take a walk around the block, and another twenty minutes doing some other relaxing, refocusing, or calming activity.

Now, let's take the Bonus Hour and bring it up a notch to a Bonus Day. My dear friend, Judy Fairchild, who was battling cancer, was in much daily pain and hated for her son to see her that way. Yet, she felt that every day with him was a Bonus Day. What if we lived everyday as if it were a Bonus Day? The reality is that we are not promised an extra hour, day, or year. What we have, and always have had through the centuries, is this moment in time…literally! Can you imagine the mindfulness, presence, calm, and love that would permeate everyone and every conversation? At the end of the day, Why Not?

BE Bold

Every person I interviewed for this book took bold action. They stay focused on the end goal. They make sure they take some action, no matter how small, in the direction they want to go, because they know the importance of keeping the movement, action going forward.

Here are a few BE bold muscles they built up and flex regularly:

Meditation—Generation Why Notter David Meltzer, sports agent and performance coach says, when he started meditating, he was able to come up with answers to questions that, before, did not come easily. He also said that he wakes up every morning at 4 a.m. so he has time to be present and start his day with meditation and exercise.

Many people say they don't know how to meditate. Quite honestly, I believe there is not only one way to do this. The most important thing to remember is to just BE and allow your mind to rest from thoughts and worry. And start slowly until you feel more comfortable with the process. I personally can't meditate sitting in a chair for more than ten minutes.

Visualization—There is so much research today on the brain and how visualization works. When you visualize your goals and dreams as already having them, there is cognitive dissonance between your subconscious mind and what is real or present for you today. In other words, as you continue daily to visualize your dreams as though they already exist with the strong appropriate feelings that go with it, then your subconscious mind…taking all cues from your thoughts and feelings…starts to believe it to be true. As a result, you are now attracting the energy vibration of what you want versus what you don't want. Your brain starts to create new neural pathways to accommodate for these new thoughts and beliefs!! I find it truly fascinating. Then, energy of the natural bounty of the Universe and Synchronicity joins in to make your experience more abundant than you thought possible. Athletes have known this for decades. They know that visualization enhances the confidence and talents in reaching their goals, no pun intended.

Again, it's important to remember that your subconscious doesn't know what is real or not real. It takes its cues from you, your perceptions, and attitude. So, if you want to have more money, it would be a good thing to visualize you receiving large sums of money and what you'll do with it. Most people, however, visualize and think of the lack of money, and that is what will expand. Remember, it's about living where you want to live rather than where you are at this moment. Why is that so important? Because our life today is made up of our thoughts and beliefs from yesterday. If you want to change your today and future, your words and beliefs must be consistent with what you want, not with what you don't want…starting *now*!

Affirmation—The subconscious doesn't know reality from fiction. This is the primary reason you want to add Affirmations to your daily action routine. Plus, when I hear myself saying I CAN do something, it inspires me to keep moving in that positive direction…it is self-motivating. When I say things to myself in my thoughts that are critical, then that is demotivating and does not inspire me to keep moving forward or be in the flow of high vibrational energy. In fact, self-criticism or any destructive criticism is demotivating.

Persistence—It is often said that the sole difference between those who succeed and those who don't is the former group kept going one more time! Or another way to look at it is that the person who did not succeed stopped one too short!

I would call Jack Canfield and Mark Victor Hansen, coauthors of the multimillion-dollar Chicken Soup book brand, the poster people for persistence. If they had stopped looking for a publisher to publish their first *Chicken Soup for the Soul* book, history would probably be very different. But they persisted through more than a hundred rejections from publishers. It took only one little publisher to say, "Yes," and that "little" publisher is no longer small.

BE curious—A wonderful way to stay out of judgment is to be curious. Curiosity is the mother of creative invention. Plus, it has you communicating and working with others out of curiosity rather than judging them for who they are or what they say. This is essential in any type of business or relationship.

Stay "hungry" to learning, to dreaming, and to possibility—all the people I interviewed for this book, *Generation Why Not?*®, had a passion for learning, dreaming, and possibility. They actually used these words when speaking.

*Make the hard decisions…*the ones that others are afraid to make, and you know they need to be made. A true leader is one who can make the hard decisions and not worry what others will say or think. They make these decisions for the greater good of the business and its stakeholders, not only its shareholders.

Four Daily Rituals

The interesting thing about rituals is that they relax and refresh. And you know what happens when you refresh: you're more apt to take clear action. I would recommend four daily rituals. If you only do one or two, that works as well.

Mornings

Here is what I do that makes all the difference for me, many of my clients, and for many of the members of Generation Why Not?® I interviewed.

1. I have a morning ritual that includes making coffee and sitting quietly with a pen and notebook and just allowing my mind to wander. What happens is that I end up planning my whole day, and now I don't worry if I haven't written down something because, in this state of Being and allowing anything to come up, clarity, next steps, and solutions come forward that amaze me.

2. Create your own morning ritual, even if it's only for ten to fifteen minutes. It's a wonderful way to start the day.

3. Keep your mornings as positive as you can, as your mornings set the stage for the day psychologically and energetically!

4. If you need to wake up fifteen minutes earlier, then do it…whatever it takes to have quiet time for yourself and allow yourself to think and BE. It is often said that Warren Buffet spends most of his time in quietude thinking, planning, and strategizing. He knows the power of personal quiet time.

After Lunch

The body is working to digest your food, and your brain is not as alert, as the body is doing its job. This is usually a lower-energy time, and there needs to be a bit of a transition after lunch and getting back to focused work. That's what we're always looking to achieve…focused work ends up being more effective and smarter, and takes less energy and time.

1. This is a great time to visualize working efficiently on the next important task or project for the afternoon.
2. Think of what you were able to accomplish in the morning and use that as a diving board to accomplishing projects in the afternoon.
3. Drink a lot of water to stay hydrated. Dehydration can bring on headaches, sluggishness, and unnecessary exhaustion.

Transition between Work and Home

For those of you who have children at home, you know how important this one is to your sanity! I remember coming home from work and my oldest child, Naomi, would start asking me questions and want all my attention. I was tired, and all I wanted to do was to go to my room upstairs and get into something more comfortable before coming back downstairs to make dinner. Here's how I handled it:

1. I shared with my daughter that "Mom needs ten minutes of personal time before I can be completely available for you and...."
2. In the car, I took an additional ten minutes to leave work behind and change to a grateful, yet tired, space of family time.

Before Bed

About an hour or so before bed is a very important time to change gears and start relaxing. There's always taking a relaxing bath, reading something positive, watching a funny movie or skit…or just sipping hot chamomile tea and enjoying the quiet. One of the main reasons that people have a difficult time falling asleep at night is because their mind is still on the day's overdrive. Thinking of stressful things will also put your mind in overdrive and make it more difficult to relax and go to sleep. Create a special bedtime ritual that works for you.

If the Energy of Action Could Talk, It Would Say…

"I'm all around you and I'm ready to move forward if you allow me to, but your self-limiters and your fear of being judged and not good enough or smart enough just gets in the way.

"I'm here ready and willing to get you where you want to go, if you'd just get out of the way and let me do my magic. The next time you're feeling human, I just want you to remember why you want me around and then just make it happen. I never leave you; it's just that your blind spots sometimes can't see me, and you feel stuck. I never take a break…I'm moving all the time. You just need to get on for the ride, and I'll take you where you want to go. I'm abundant and everywhere…you can't miss me, if you're truly looking for me, rather than getting stuck in your own thoughts."

Generation Why Not?® Breakthrough Bonus Download #5
Time and Money Breakthrough Exercises
Bonus download here: www.ruthklein.com/why-not-bonuses

Meditation on Increasing Time and Money
Listen to it here: www.ruthklein.com/why-not-bonuses

Song that captures the essence of the chapter:
"It's My Life" by Bon Jovi

CHAPTER 9

QUANTUM SYNCHRONICITY®
PRINCIPLE #6:
THE SECRET ENERGY OF MOMENTUM

"Life is like riding a bicycle. To keep your
balance you must keep moving."
Albert Einstein

Nothing happens without first taking action...even the
smallest amount of action taken can start the momentum.
And our personal vibrational energy is such that we first
need to BE the very thing we want to see manifested on the outside. Remember, your outer experiences are a reflection of your
inner reality. So, if you want to have a more passionate or peaceful romantic relationship, you must create that Intention within
yourself first. If you want your management teams to be more

productive and communicative, you must create that Intention within yourself first. If you want a more financially prosperous business, you must create that Intention within yourself first without any Paradoxical (or competing) Intentions. Otherwise, because of its energetic nature, the Universe will be frenetic for you.

Through research, interviews, and my experiences with clients, I've discovered there are four key factors of momentum, driven by Quantum Synchronicity®: movement, commitment, engagement, and visualization. Engagement shows up in many different areas of our lives. And the level of engagement is directly correlative to the amount of momentum we feel from each factor. Let's look at each one a little more closely.

How the Physics of Momentum
Applies to Business Success

Quantum Physics shows that your energy expands in the world and has influence locally and nonlocally. Every energetic vibration has an impact on everything else within your own life: your business, communications, health, and community, as well as the world at large.

In other words, your personal energetic vibration becomes the powerhouse that expands all around you and within you. You are so much more powerful than you realize, and it is this influence that plays a direct role on your business and life…and those around you, near as well as far away.

Because of these vast opportunities and our nonlocal power, I encourage you to always continue to take action in the direction of your goals. The results may not come in the manner you expect, but with the right energy, they will come about just the same. And those results may, in fact, be better than you could have imagined.

Generation Why Notter Andrea Albright had to basically start all over with her online fitness, health, and lifestyle programs after her divorce. She felt completely demotivated and uncertain as to what the next step to take should be after spending years working with her ex-husband on the business. Now Andrea was left with, as she says, "nothing to show for it."

However, at some point, she realized that her passion, her Big Why, and her intellectual property (her resources and the knowledge of her previous work) were in alignment, and this motivated Andrea to take inspired action.

She found the right team and started from scratch, with a limited amount of money but a boundless passion! Within two years, her online fitness company was estimated to be worth $250 million! Andrea says, "In no way could I even have imagined this level of success, especially when I felt so devastated." She goes on to say, "Thank God, I never gave up. All this just made me want it even more, and I knew I could do it, even though I was so scared and had limited funds."

How Quantum Synchronicity® Applies
to Momentum Movement

Nothing happens without first taking action…even the smallest amount of action taken can start the momentum going. It's about allowing the Quantum Universe to lend its magical energy to match your energy. Andrea was able to look in several directions, such as finding the right team, attracting investors, drawing on the confidence from her previous successes, rekindling her "can-do" attitude, moving to less expensive city to save on costs, and much more. By taking action in several directions, she was able to expand her energy and momentum, allowing Quantum Synchronicity® to do its magic. Andrea kept working on several options, which prompted her to keep going and looking for new avenues for success.

Andrea kept up the momentum by taking small actions in the direction of the dream she envisioned. This type of momentum took her out of feeling overwhelmed and allowed her to be the living vibration of what I call the "Miracle Field." Remember those times when you were feeling so good, on a natural high, and things were just flowing for you? That is the living vibration of the Miracle Field. I would say that this state of clarity and tranquility is where things are flowing and evidence that all your cylinders are firing: Intentions, Thoughts, Beliefs, Decisions, and Actions are in alignment, and you feel so much momentum. This flow of alignment is what Quantum Synchronicity® feels like in action. It definitely is real and shows up when all the vibrational gears are activated at a high level. And here's the best part:

You have the power to make it happen by controlling only those things you can—your Intentions, Thoughts, Beliefs, Decisions, Actions, Momentum, and Environment. From there, allow Quantum Synchronicity® to join you and turn the "impossible" into what's possible. Unfortunately, this vibrational energy can also work in the opposite direction against what you're wanting. Unless you're very clear with your Intentions, the Universe gets confused with several different competing messages between what you consciously want and what your subconscious is thinking and believing, which may be counter to what you truly want. You can look at it as something negative, or you can view "what's happening" as feedback:

1. Review your Intentions, Thoughts, Beliefs, Decisions, and Actions. By doing so, you will have a very good idea of the resistance.
2. A Paradoxical Belief may be driving the inaction or the results you don't want.
3. Big Resistance may be showing its head. This is the perfect time to be present and ask Resistance, "What do you want me to know?"

All this feedback is truly a gift! I know it doesn't feel that way at first. However, once you start to "see" life through a new lens of Quantum Synchronicity®, where you *know* things happen *for* you rather than against you, you start looking at feedback as interesting clues. By being present to these clues and paying attention to them in a way that moves you forward, rather than feeling overwhelmed or stopping you from moving forward, your life becomes a beautiful and magical journey and experience!

Commitment—Commitment to move the energy in the direction you want. Commitment has two parts: self-commitment and a shared commitment with others. Self-commitment is where you make a decision, you take action, and you commit to keep the momentum going. Self-commitment builds self-confidence and a certain type of internal integrity that allows you to be able to depend on yourself to follow up with what you set out to do.

David Klein, co-founder of CommonBond, is a case in point. He started his company with a one-to-one social mission: for every degree fully funded on the platform, CommonBond funds the education of a child in need. At one point early in the company's history, there was resistance to the idea of a social mission at scale. But David insisted, saying: "Our social mission is a part of who we are."

The commitment to others sometimes comes more easily than our commitment to ourselves. But, be that as it may, the commitment we create between ourselves and others is what keeps the relationship working. It enhances the feeling of reciprocity that you can depend on their word to do something, just as they can take your word that you'll do what you say. Both of these types of commitment add momentum to whatever you are doing or saying.

Engagement—Engagement is about connecting and, in many cases, reconnecting. Let's look at a few ways to connect in order to move forward:

- Self-Engagement—Taking pause, thinking. Reconnecting to yourself, your thoughts, your inner guidance versus feeling separate or alone and not connected in any way. Recommitting to yourself as the authentic, talented, resourceful, courageous, and loving essence of who you are.

- Home Engagement—This is the perfect time to reconnect with your home and those things in, and areas of, your home that bring you peace and put a smile on your face.

- Client Engagement—Connecting with your client onboarding. What do you do when your client starts working with you? How do you develop a client's or customer's life value? It's always less expensive to keep a client or customer than to make a new one.

- Business Engagement—When was the last time you reviewed your Best Practices for your business, your profit/loss sheets, your marketing messages, the relevancy and transparency of your business brand, the internal culture between departments, teams, and employees?

- Marketing Engagement—Reconnecting with your powerful message for all your stakeholders—clients, vendors, associates, shareholders, and others.

- Money Engagement—Money loves attention, and one of the best ways to pay money attention is to track it daily…whether it's five dollars or tens of thousands of dollars.

- Time Engagement—Time doesn't like to be rushed. So that means you're not beating the clock, because, if you do, then you will lose. Rather, it's about being conscious and present. And, in this conscious state, take inspired action and plan out your day with time blocking (as shared in Chapter 9, "The Secret Energy of Action").

- Health Engagement—Connecting with your health requires you to stay present to what your body is telling you. One of the most amazing things about our bodies is that they speak to us. Gently, at first, and then it seems to get louder and louder.

  - If you're tired, plan to get sleep and rest. And, if you don't feel you have enough time, then take time away from eating, but not sleep. It seems like we always have time to eat.

  - If your back is hurting, pay attention. Ask it, "What does this uncomfortable feeling or pain want to say to me?" Many years ago, I was in a nonsupportive relationship and stayed in it far too long. I ended up having back pain. When I asked the pain what it was trying to tell me, this is what it told me: "You can *emotionally support and nurture* yourself." Even though this man did not emotionally support or nurture me, I misinterpreted his presence in my life as being something I would really miss and stayed in the relationship way too long. And my body was loving enough to remind me daily!! Shortly after we split, I forgot about my back because there wasn't any more pain there!!

- If communications in your business relationships end up with angry comments, pay attention. It's not the time to get upset with yourself or the other person. It is simply feedback that needs to be addressed. When you find there's a pattern—something that keeps repeating, whether it's difficulties in communicating, regularly paying late fees, being late more times than being on time, losing out on promotions regularly, feeling upset a lot of the time, or blaming others for upsetting you—these experiences are all feedback that requires reconnection to some area of your life…whether it's internal or external. Remember, your *outer experiences are a reflection of your internal reality.*

Your vibrational energy influences your momentum, including the people in it. And their vibrational energy influences you. In fact, all our interactions, including with ourselves, are the ebb and flow of an energy exchange. This moving energy has a tendency to gain momentum, and it is the common denominator of our thoughts and emotions all day long. This is where Quantum Theory shows up for us. Because of how the vibrational energy influences and interacts with each other, we easily and often take on the energy of another person…from thoughts, emotions, and even physical interactions. It is a type of "entanglement" between the people and the environment within which you interact. Even after you physically leave a person, you can take on their vibrational energy. This phenomenon so riled Albert Einstein that he called it "spooky action at a distance."

Visualization—Taking the time to visualize each Quantum Synchronicity® principle will offer you clarity…the secret energy of momentum! Quantum Physics tells us, through the energy of sheer observation, that what happens in one area has a direct effect in a distant location—this quantum movement can be detected at the smallest (quantum) level. Psychologists say that what you focus on expands. You focus on what's working, and that expands. Conversely, if you focus on things that upset you and don't feel are working out the way you want them to, you seem to get more of the same. It's about taking action that moves you closer to your goals in business and life. This is where visualization becomes a beautiful way to "see" what you want and "feel" the feeling you want to achieve with that goal. Athletes have been performing this visualization for decades with a high degree of success.

When you do this visualization, you're actually creating the quantum energy of "expectancy theory," or a self-fulfilling prophecy. Basically, that which you talk about and believe is going to happen will…once you've set up the energetic pattern, whether it's what you do or don't want!!

James, a top television celebrity who had been away from a major network for six years, was feeling rejected and frustrated. Our coaching work together changed his Intention, Thoughts, Beliefs, and Decisions to reflect on what he wanted, rather than on how demotivated he felt. Within three and a half months, he was offered the opportunity to host a show on a major network!! This was his recent text message to me: "Are you sitting down? I'm beginning to believe you make miracles happen in people's lives. Here's why…I found out that a major network wants me back on my show." The truth is that James found himself in the Miracle Field, with all cylinders firing and the stars in alignment…literally!

James is the one who created the "miracle" inside the Universal energy of Quantum Synchronicity®. And I know you can create miracles in your life too!

So, if this is true, then why wouldn't you want to visualize what you truly want? If you have the opportunity and the gift to write or rewrite your story, wouldn't you want to be the main character who reaches your dreams? C'mon…this is your time!! Be the protagonist of your own novel! Allow the gift of momentum to help you!

Why not allow the Universal energy of Quantum Synchronicity® to work to your benefit and energetically influence the success of your dreams?

Are you ready to start living in the Miracle Field?

Momentum Energy Drainers

It's important to be present to the energy drainers that exist all around you. And the moment you feel "out of sorts," self-doubt, exhausted after sleeping, in an angry or upset mood, or any other non-harmonious thoughts or feelings, you may want to see what momentum energy drainer lurks nearby.

Here are a few of the ones to be "present" to. In other words, be open to the feedback, refocus, recommit, and visualize the scenario you desire, and move forward. Period!

Burnout—When you feel totally exhausted, you are in full burnout mode. Burnout is very similar to dehydration. When you feel thirsty, you are already dehydrated!! And what do you do to stay hydrated? Keep drinking water. What do you do to avoid burnout? You make sure you are present to your vibrational energy and protect it from energy drainers. You pause or stop and nurture yourself…it's time to regenerate and refill your own energy container.

Boundary issues, especially with time and money—Giving your time away to others and then feeling overwhelmed with all that you have to do. The same applies to money. James would give any of his friends money when they asked for it. They said they would pay him back, but the truth is…they took their time… sometimes as long as years, or never. That ended up making James feel overwhelmed by money issues.

Overwhelm—If you're feeling overwhelmed most of the time, this can be great feedback. There are reasons why we feel the way we feel. And that's a good thing. However, many of us continue to keep the energy drainers without checking them out and doing something about them. Do you want to know the best way to pull out of feeling overwhelmed within five minutes or less? Make a list of what needs to be done and then choose *one* task and do it. Taking action in the direction you desire pulls you out of the overwhelm zone and gets you into momentum! And, before you know it, you're focused. Continue doing this until you feel completely out of overwhelm and in clarity.

Exhaustion—Getting good sleep is underestimated. Many times, busy people think the only way to add more time to their day is to wake up earlier and sleep less. I can tell you from experience, as well as what the research on productivity and health says: getting seven to eight hours of sleep nightly gives your mind and body a chance to rest, reset, and reenergize. Here's the deal: once you start being present to how you're feeling and visualizing what you want, you will save hours daily from obsessing, worrying, feeling overwhelmed, or some form of self-doubt, anxiety, or worry.

And, if you do experience any of these energy drainers, know this is just feedback. Going through the Seven Principles of Quantum Synchronicity® will bring you back to balance and momentum, and once again you'll feel confident you can move forward. This is exactly what the majority of Generation Why Notters do daily….and sometimes hourly, depending on what's going on.

Draining Relationships—Yes, this is the time to let go of draining relationships with gratitude. They came into your life for a reason or a season. You know the ones…who put you in an uncomfortable position, where you feel you're on the defensive; who don't support you; who are dramatizers; those friends who put you down under the "umbrella" of "just kidding."

I know it may not be easy, but it's definitely necessary. This is an opportunity for you to flex your courage and self-commitment muscles! Generation Why Notter Tanya Memme, Emmy nominated TV host and host of A&E's television show, *Sell This House*, says, "Actually, it wasn't difficult at all. Once I made the decision to support myself and only be with supportive people, it came easily. I felt so good and in complete integrity when I did let the draining relationships go."

More Energy Drainers Hijacking Your Momentum

Among the biggest energy-draining culprits that can hijack our good Intentions toward moving forward are boundaries. Below are a few boundaries that can drain your momentum. And it's important to note that consistently failing to keep healthy boundaries becomes a pattern and usually shows up in other areas of your life, including business, personal life, money, and time, to name a few. Here is a more inclusive list around bound-aries—time-draining tasks that distract and take you off your primary focus and often derail you and your team:

- Debt
- No control of your time
- No control of your money
- Clutter
- Discounting what you charge before being asked to do so
- Trading services
- Stacks of papers
- Incomplete projects
- Negative friends or family members
- Always taking care of others
- Taking clients with consistent payment challenges
- High drama around money or time
- Charging far less than others just to get the client/job
- Not following up with potential clients/customers

- Excessive worrying
- Fear of rejection
- Fear of failure/success
- Fear of not enough money
- Fear of judgment
- High level of anxiety—test anxiety, performance anxiety
- Putting things off to the very last minute
  (aka procrastination)

Feeling Stuck?

Are you ready to get some understanding regarding what happens when you're feeling "stuck," stagnant, not moving forward, not taking the next right action, and you don't know why? Let's go through the process of getting clarity, so you can gain momentum. Remember, the secret energy of momentum is clarity.

We often hear the expression "Your heart isn't in it." In many ways, that is exactly what's happening. You've disconnected from your Big Why…and from your authentic Self.

Here's a recent situation I found myself experiencing while going through the process of writing this book. The following example will help you move forward on those days and times when you've had a tough day, heard one too many no's, or you just don't have the mojo or energy to keep up the momentum.

Intention: Write an impactful book for the reader and invite them to a new perceptual paradigm for creating a life full of passion, purpose, and alignment in business and in life.

Paradoxical Intention: Not that I've identified.

Thought: I'm excited to get this information out and share it, so that we can start a conversation about these ideas on a large scale.

Paradoxical Thought: But...there's so much to write about. Where do I even start? I have a book proposal with bullet topics for each chapter, but they're not feeling right for this manuscript now.

Belief: The conversation around Generation Why Not?® is a game changer for a new way to see, communicate, and act in business, with community, and in life.

Paradoxical Belief: This is reallllly big...I'm not sure I can get all of it into this book. I could actually write a book on each chapter. "I'm filled to the brim with information and examples."

Decision: I've checked off writing sessions to write this book within the next three months.

Paradoxical Decision: I kept putting writing off because "I am so busy." And, as the publishing date nears, I'm getting anxious.

Action: I'm going to spend Fridays, Saturdays, Sundays, and Mondays, from 7:00 a.m. to noon, writing.

Paradoxical Action: "I have too much to do this morning." Or it sounded like this on Saturday or Sunday: "I need a weekend day to just relax."

Momentum: I have enough time to complete this book with the schedule I've laid out. I've written six books before using a book proposal, and this book will flow as well.

Paradoxical Momentum: Feeling overwhelmed with the wealth of information I want to share. "How do I organize all this so that it makes sense and flows? I've never had this issue with other books I've written. What's going on?"

If you've been following me on Instagram, you would see several posts where I shared my dismay and surprise during the writing of this book.

Clarity: "I am trying to get two decades of learning, insights, and experiences into one book. Oh, wow, that is why it makes organizing the information so difficult. There's too much, and I'm overwhelming myself. OK…I can do this!! I will focus on the important points for each chapter. Done!"

Intention: Same as above.

Thought: "I will organize each chapter by important points and then allow the writing to flow. I've got this."

Belief: "I can do this!!"

Decision: I will sequester myself out of town, so the only things I have to do are write, service my clients, eat, walk, and sleep… that's it!

Action: Set a goal of writing one chapter every two to three writing sessions.

Momentum: I reengaged with the essence of my "Big Why" in writing this book to begin with. I made a commitment to myself that I can do this and do it within the time frame. I focused on only one chapter at a time and reconnected with each topic chapter.

I did move forward in a big way and with great momentum, although I did need to ask for three writing extensions. I've never needed a writing extension before. All I can say is, "Acceptance of what is, is humbling."

Momentum Energy Supporters

Have *fun*…making time just for fun; making time for something you enjoy. "Just because" helps lift our energy. I know I have to "plan" for my "fun" momentum energy supporters or they won't happen! Here's a list of some momentum energy supporters that we know would help, but sometimes we forget they're available:

Being with a community of people you enjoy
Music, especially uplifting beats
Gratitude
Exercise
Dancing
Sports
Good conversation
Loving relationships

Strategies for Momentum "Reengagement"

Business: Mind, Body, and Spirit

Mind—Focus and follow up.
Body—Refocus on your Intentions and Thoughts after lunch.
Spirit—Stay positive, look for the feedback "gift."

Family: Mind, Body, and Spirit

Mind—Peace and harmony

Body—Loving boundaries
Spirit—Gratitude

Friends: Mind, Body, and Spirit

Mind—Acceptance of "perfect imperfections"
Body—Respect for myself and others
Spirit—Abundance and fun

Home: Mind, Body, and Spirit

Mind—Organization and letting go of clutter
Body—Nurturing home
Spirit—Acceptance and gratitude

Time: Mind, Body, and Spirit

Mind—Consciousness and being Present
Body—I "get" to… versus I "have" to….
Spirit—Gratitude for the time you have each day

Money: Mind, Body, and Spirit

Mind—Abundance and existing wealth
Body—Visualization and joy
Spirit—Abundance and gratitude

Health: Mind, Body, and Spirit

Mind—Visualizing health and vitality

Body—Intense self-nurturing

Spirit—Loving and letting go of anything else

The Silent Energy of Successful Momentum

In order to create momentum, some type of energy needs to be activated. Plus, this energy also works best when it's on a higher vibration, which is the positive type of energy that pulls us forward and motivates us to do something. Momentum begets momentum and only requires quantum (small) action steps. The silent energy of successful momentum is clarity. Clarity of your purpose, clarity of your Big Why, clarity of your Intentions, clarity of your dreams, clarity of your goals, clarity of the next right step, and clarity of visualization of what you want and how you want to feel. And, then, allow the energy of the Universe and Quantum Synchronicity® to work its magic!

Momentum Mindset for Moving Forward

I wanted to share my list of Intentions to help you keep up your Momentum. Feel free to use them as your own, if you so desire.

- Choose Faith over Fear in all situations and with all thoughts.
- I am a multimillion-dollar CEO of my business with impeccable boundaries and integrity.

- I only work with my ideal clients.
- I actively engage with my team.
- I spend time daily in full appreciation for my gifts and talents.
- I am grateful for everything that shows up in my life.
- I co-create the business and the life of my dreams.
- I'm living my life as a love story to the Universe.
- Clarity and commitment move me forward.
- I keep my focus on the bigger vision.

Generation Why Not?® Breakthrough Bonus Download #6
20 Ways to Leverage Momentum Checklist
Bonus download here: www.ruthklein.com/why-not-bonuses

Meditation on Staying Motivated & Engaged
Listen to it here: www.ruthklein.com/why-not-bonuses

Song that captures the essence of the chapter:
"Fight Song" by Rachel Platten

CHAPTER 10

QUANTUM SYNCHRONICITY® PRINCIPLE #7: THE SECRET ENERGY OF ENVIRONMENT

"Success is peace of mind, which is a direct result of self-satisfaction in knowing you made the effort to become the best of which you are capable."
Coach John Wooden

Our environment plays a large role in how we live our lives. In so many ways, it is the intangibility of our environment that has the greatest energetic effect on us, even though we may be unaware of it. The intangibility of your environment is the energy and perception we give it. We can't really see this "energy," but we definitely feel it. The energy exists, and the perception of our environment creates positive or negative feelings.

And these internal environmental factors are your team of energy supporters or energy drainers…it's all in the way you perceive and give meaning to them. So the environment directly impacts you subliminally and energetically.

Let's look at three different environments: the biological, the internal, and the external (physical).

Your Biological Environment

I find biology to be so interesting, especially after reading and listening to Dr. Bruce Lipton, a stem cell biologist and author of the book *The Biology of Belief.* Dr. Lipton was instrumental in discovering the science of epigenetics, which explores the cellular chemical reactions that switch our genes on or off. In his research, he goes further, saying that our environmental perceptions of events in our lives have a more powerful influence on our health than drugs do. Another way to look at these findings is that we have an innate opportunity and capacity to heal ourselves that exceeds the influence of pharmaceutical drugs.

Why is this research so important? According to Dr. Lipton, the old biology regarded us as victims. And victims lose the motivation to make changes, thinking, *What's the use?* Instead, Dr. Lipton says this new biological research states that, if we can change our perceptions, we can change the outcomes of our cells and health. In fact, his research suggests that the cell membrane is the cell's brain, and it is here where each cell receives environmental signals. The receptor proteins pick up emotions of love or any other emotion and is primary in creating a healthy or unhealthy biological environment. And how do the receptor proteins know how to interpret the emotion? We interpret the emotion as we perceive it, based on our beliefs! If we change our beliefs to those that are life-serving and high vibrational energy (positive energy is of a high vibration) rather than the lower vibrational energy of emotions such as anxiety, anger, and jealousy, we'll be healthier.

Looking through an Old Lens

With the information provided by the research of Dr. Bruce Lipton, how do you start looking at your health and stress levels through a new lens? The first place I suggest you consider turning to is the Seven Principles of Quantum Synchronicity®. When you're feeling any type of upset, go through the Seven Principles and try and do the exercise at the end of each chapter, as well as more online with the Bonus Downloads.

This is how a client, James, identified his upset, was able to look through a new lens, and found he was able to sleep again without waking up with anxiety attacks.

Intention: To create a new and successful career coaching entrepreneurs using his video and camera presentation skills.
Paradoxical Intention: I would also love to have a career again on television. They do all the work, and I just show up and do my thing. It's easy for me.
Thought: I can help entrepreneurs with their external presentation and brand. I'm excited to be doing this.

Paradoxical Thought: "I don't really know how to coach. I don't even know how to set all this up or where to start."

Belief: I've been doing video production and camera work for over two decades, and I enjoy it very much.

Paradoxical Belief: It feels like going from a real profession to do coaching in this area—seems like I'm a failure at doing video production and camera work for TV.

Decision: OK, I'll start putting some information together to let entrepreneurs know what I do and a start date for a group or private class.

Paradoxical Decision: I'm not really committed 100 percent to this career change.

Action: He went through the motions of putting together written material that was quite good, although he was waking up at night with the sweats, experiencing panic attacks.

Paradoxical Action: Procrastination looks like: 1) What is it again I need to do? I forgot; 2) Changed his mind once again about what and how he'll be doing it; 3) He moved residences; and 4) He left for a planned vacation out of the country for three weeks.

Momentum: Start, stop; start, stop.

Paradoxical Momentum: His heart wasn't in it, and he was not passionate about it.

Environment: Perfect timing…His home lease was up, and James moved to a much smaller place, although the environment was so much "happier" and "positive."

Paradoxical Environment: He had clutter and boxes for weeks at the new residence, where he couldn't find things and felt frazzled.

Looking through a New Lens

Intention: To create a profitable business that I love and that helps other entrepreneurs through video and camera presentation coaching. And, I would love to have a television show again.

Thought: "I have a lot I can share with my clients to make their social media and presentations more impactful to attract customers."

Belief: "I can do this, and I've been doing this type of thing for decades."

Decision: "I'm doing this and not letting everyday 'life' stop me as an excuse. Full steam ahead."

Action: Made a commitment to go forward, stayed focused on what the needed steps were, and moved forward each day, one small step at a time.

Momentum: "I'm enjoying the moment! So much hasn't made sense in the last year, so I'm going with what does make sense!"

Environment: James created a schedule that works and allows him to be present with his young daughter late in the afternoons.

Magical Outcome: Within three and a half months, James was asked to be on a national TV network doing video production and camera work on a television show and started speaking and coaching on his new career extension.

What Are You Tolerating?

One of the most productive ways to gauge our environmental energy is to become aware of the things, people, and places that upset us. And, in that place of upset, think of all the things you are tolerating, even though they may be draining your energy and peace of mind.

Let's look at what James was tolerating: negative people, disrespectful behavior from dating partners and friends, potential business partners who called the shots and aggressively took control of the situation. He tolerated friends not paying him back when they said they would. He tolerated people being judgmental and critical of his ideas, decisions, and thoughts.

Letting Go with Gratitude

Tanya Memme says about letting go of things no longer serving her, "I feel like I've had a second chance in so many ways. When making better decisions becomes a priority, and letting go of decisions that didn't serve me, it's amazing how things changed. One of the best decisions I made was to open up more and appreciate even the small things that bless my life daily."

Your Internal Environment

Your internal environment is the most impactful on your peace of mind, momentum, success, and overall health. Let's look at how Quantum Synchronicity® and the Seven Principles help with creating a balanced and happy internal environment.

The Seven "Environments" of Quantum Synchronicity®

Intentions—Become an *observer* of the motivation behind what you want and think, and how you'd like the results to be…for the greater good of all the people it affects. Intentions that are pure, loving, clear, and passionate are the ones that help keep you motivated in the direction of what you want. Your Intention sets up the energetic vibration for your day, for your project, for your relationships, or anything else where you consciously create what you want. Changing your Intentions to something positive and passionate for you is the first step.

Thoughts—Observe your words and the feelings that come from your thoughts. You can do this when you're with other people, during work, during a movie, when you listen to the news, or anywhere your thoughts take you. Your thoughts are your first line of defense. Your thoughts start to activate your emotions and feelings that will energize or drain you. It is often said—and I definitely believe it—that once you change your thoughts, you change your life. That is how powerful you are. And, by allowing for the good to enter your life, you attract the Universal energy of Quantum Synchronicity®.

Generation Why Notter Sydney, a high-octane twenty-something social media entrepreneur, says, "I tell my mom how I manifest everything I desire, and she's now interested in knowing what that means. But you've got to be so pure in your Intention…it can't be against anyone—it needs to be for the greater good."

Beliefs—"Cleaning up" and updating who you are today. Since most of our beliefs were "inherited" when we were between the ages of two to eight from our family, with the cognitive understanding of a child, we now have the opportunity to do what I like to refer to as a "reality check" on our beliefs. And the treasure in finding out what those beliefs are is identifying what is limiting you. Almost always, we limit ourselves because of our beliefs about how we see ourselves—confident or not, good enough or not, smart or not, attractive or not, desirable or not.... OK, you get the picture, and now you can let go of the old, useless, disempowering belief and create a new empowering and more *real* and *truthful* belief about yourself today. You are in control of your new story and how you want it to look, feel, and be experienced!!

Decisions—Your decisions are crucial to the outcome of your life. But here's the catch: your decisions are directly impacted by your beliefs. And your commitment to yourself, your growth, and how you want to live your life are all available to you...now! In fact, every day you have the opportunity to commit and make a decision that is life-serving for you. It requires courage and commitment to living the life you truly desire in business, in relationships, in your community, and with your health.

Actions—Nothing happens without taking some kind of action in the direction of your dreams and goals. If you find you're not taking action, or your action is not producing the results you want, this is the perfect time to identify the thoughts you're telling yourself, the beliefs behind the thoughts, and the decisions you're making. This information is a treasure trove for your moving forward. You become the private investigator of your own life. You have the opportunity to connect with what is true and what is not true for you. Taking action has nothing to do with anything external to you; the economy, your surroundings, your past experiences, waiting for others, or a special time to act…all these "excuses" are resistance speaking to you. And, if you understand the language of Quantum Synchronicity®, then you can use a very strong, high-vibrational, invisible energy to assist you.

At the end of the day, you're not alone. You have the Universal Consciousness, Invisible Vibrational Energy, and Your Inner GPS every second of the day. As long as you have yourself, you'll never be alone. What are you waiting for? Maybe it's time to embrace these gifts. Why Not?

Momentum—Your momentum depends on your internal environment and has nothing to do with your external environment. It's so easy to "blame" others, the external environment, and whatever else you think is "stopping" you from moving forward. Just know that reasoning is simply resistance to getting started or maintaining energy. The first place you want to "research" and get information as to why you may be procrastinating is: What is your Intention (or Thoughts, Beliefs, Decisions) around this task, call, email, project? Once you identify the real reason for your resistance, you will find yourself moving forward again.

Environment—Your environment can easily be divided into three main areas: 1) Biological Environment; 2) Internal Environment; and 3) External Environment. And, at the end of the day, the two environments that have the most power are Biological and Internal.

Let's look at Angela's internal environment and the impact it made on her life for over thirty years!!

Looking through the Old Lens

Intention: Angela, a new children's book author and illustrator, wanted to market her children's book to inspire children's self-esteem.

Paradoxical Intention: I spent tens of thousands of dollars for marketing help, and nothing happened. I'm skeptical that I won't be able to find another marketing person to help me with my children's book.

Thought: I'm in need of a marketing person.

Paradoxical Thought: How can I trust whomever I hire next to be honest with me?

Belief: I want to sell more of my children's book.

Paradoxical Belief: I don't really know how to do that. What am I going to do?

Decision: I hired a book marketing coach (I was the person she hired).

Paradoxical Decision: I hope she does what she says she's going to do for my book.

Action: Angela started to create a foundational marketing system with database software, inserting names and emails into the database and other tasks.

Paradoxical Action: What does all this have to do with marketing my book?

Momentum: She kept up with all the marketing strategies I suggested to her and was feeling a kind of confidence she had never felt before.

Paradoxical Momentum: Every so often, Angela would doubt herself and what she was doing, and it would slow her down a bit.

Environment: I only want to work the months that won't infringe on my vacations and holidays with my husband and family.

Paradoxical Environment: Angela has kept true to her word.

Looking through the New Lens

Intention: Creating a business around my book with many profitable strategies.

Thought: I feel like a new person after decades of giving my artwork away. I finally feel like I have the career I've always wanted and am having fun in it.

Belief: I'm increasing my confidence daily starting my new career, meeting new people, and doing things I never thought I could do…and I'm doing them.

Decision: Once I knew I made the right decision with my marketing coach and the things she was saying felt right, although scary, I made the decision I would do this to the best of my ability…and I am.

Action: Follows up on all marketing strategies, taking small steps almost daily.

Momentum: Angela is getting people to contact her to speak, do art projects, and saying "yes" to her proposals.

Environment: Angela's internal environment is totally in alignment, and she makes her physical environment work, no matter if she's out fishing or away at far-flung locations. She is committed, focused, and having fun!

Magical Outcome: Within three months, Angela is getting paid for her art projects, connecting with nonprofits to help them raise funds as she gets paid to tell her story and offer a fun art project for the adult patrons, selling her book on social media, talking to children's authors about doing the illustrations for their children's books, reading her book and doing art projects in classrooms.

What Are You Tolerating in Your Internal Environment?

Angela was tolerating a limited life based on her old, disempowering story; she limited her opportunities and the possibility of coming into her own and becoming the success she felt her brothers enjoyed, but not her. She was never jealous of her brothers—in fact, she was one of their greatest fans and admirers! And yet she knew she wanted to branch out and live a big dream, helping children increase their self-esteem, but didn't know exactly what her vision was or how to go about finding it.

Letting Go with Gratitude

Angela came to the realization that she could create a solid business based on her passion of art and writing children's books. She let go, with gratitude, of the old belief of not being smart enough and found the freedom of being herself, doing what she loved doing while getting paid for it. She let go of not thinking her talents were valuable. Angela let those internal beliefs go with gratitude because she now knows that she couldn't get to her place of such appreciation, had she not experienced the other self-limiting way of being.

Your External Environment

The external environment includes outside events, other people, places, and physical areas—all that is outside of us. The external environment is neutral, and we give it meaning by how we perceive and interpret outside events, people, and physical surroundings.

What may be one person's trash is another person's treasure. This is certainly evident in thrift stores. It comes down to how we perceive our external environment. We can choose to let it drain our energy, or we can choose to allow it to elevate us to a higher energy vibration of flow.

I personally like to surround myself with "pretty." I buy a dozen fresh roses weekly and set them on my dining room table. I like living in softer colors, as they tend to be calming for me. I am grateful that I have the beautiful Pacific Ocean to enjoy, 24/7, right outside my large living room windows. Every home I have ever lived in, except for the first rented apartment when I was just married, has had a baby grand piano. At one point in my life, I was living in an apartment and I had four pieces of furniture in my living room: a couch, a table, a lamp, and a baby grand piano that took up a third of the living room. I've played piano, guitar, and violin most of my life, and the piano signified a "music center" in my home. Why? Because I gave it that meaning. To other people, it only looked like a piano in the living area.

I also like to drive without the music on…I enjoy the silence and calm. My personality is extroverted, and any time I have the opportunity to be quiet and balance my mind, I take it. At the beginning of this year, I received a Divinely Gifted Download that said, "Ruth, it's time for you to Uplevel." I then asked, "What does that even mean?" And the answer was: "It's time for you to get out of your comfort zone and show up at a higher frequency while letting go of people, places, and things that no longer serve you."

Whoa…I was so in awe and impressed with that download, as it had made a huge energetic impact on me, that I decided to host a two-day live event called "Uplevel Your Brand—Uplevel Your Business." I had a packed room, in addition to twelve product sponsors! How did that new awareness show up for me in my environment?

- I gave away two old couches and bought one gorgeous white half-circle couch that I've wanted for years!
- I threw out my twenty-year-old desk that was falling apart in places and replaced it with a gorgeous white desk with a matching white swivel chair.
- I gave away my bed headboard and bought a beautiful gray suede one, and now the colors in my bedroom are gray and pink—normally, way out of my "normal."
- I got serious about letting go of weight and started with letting go of 90 percent of the sugar I was ingesting per week.

- I lost six pounds, without really trying, within four weeks.
- I let go of my fish maintenance person because I wasn't going to tolerate his not showing up.
- I let go of the "protective need" for a car with a hard roof…I chose to buy a convertible.

What I realized, from another download, was it was time for me to stop living in my comfort zone…in my cocoon. It was time to let the outer layer go and be the butterfly I was meant to be. Or, more specifically, how I was years before my divorce! Something opened up for me in my environment…both internally and externally. I was ready to fly again. I was "wowed" by this new insight. I went on a "letting go" spree…I let go of clothes, shoes, and other stuff. It was as though some other spirit entered my body, and the external environment of things that I felt connected to before no longer existed! It was, at first, a surreal feeling. I was letting go of things and just "observing" how it didn't bother me at all!

- I cleaned out my refrigerator completely, to the point that it looked like no one was living here.
- I cleaned out and tossed old cosmetics and all the gifted cosmetics that I thought I wanted and never used.
- I gave away a living room table and haven't missed it.
- I gave away books…about a hundred of them. (OK, I have a LOT of books.)

And, as I let go of the old and those things that no longer served me, I opened up myself to a new energy that brought in a book deal (within a week of doing this, after seven months of reaching out to publishers); more public speaking opportunities showed up; I attracted my ideal clients all from referrals; and I started an Uplevel Mastermind program.

As I opened up more space in my external environment, Upleveled, and let go of the old, my home and car became less cluttered, and I allowed for new energy to come in. As I let go of each item, I thanked it for coming into my life and for its service. It may sound strange, but it was a beautiful and easier way to let go. In fact, I had held on to several pieces of my parents' furniture and gave away a few items. I never thought I would or could. When I gave them away with gratitude, it sounded like this: "You brought a lot of life and love to our family, and now I let you go so you can bring a lot of life and love to another family." At that point, I couldn't wait to share the loving energy with another family. Energetically, it felt right, and I was at peace with giving it away.

So what are you tolerating in your external environment? And are you ready to let go of those things that no longer bring you joy and to share them with others? As I gave the books to Goodwill, I was so happy knowing others would be reading great books on business, marketing, and success, while finding inspiration in them and making an impact in their lives, as many books have done for me. In fact, books are amazing in making an impact on our lives. Think of the book that had the biggest influence on your life. Or helped you make an informed and better decision. Or gave you some special insight into the lives of others. You will always find books, a piano, a violin, roses, violets, orchids, a huge dining room table and chairs, as well as a lot of pretty china and second-hand glassware, lovely stationery and cards, candles of all sizes, a plush throw over the couch, plus a bottle or two of Rombauer Zinfandel wine at my home, at all times! What can you always depend upon to surround yourself with in your environment that will put a smile on your face?

Your Money Environment

It may seem that money is external to you, but that is not entirely true. The actual physicality of money is external to you. However, your relationship to money is internal. In other words, how you perceive money in your subconscious is what drives your financial situation and your bank account.

T. Harv Eker, a multimillionaire and president of Peak Potentials Training, says: "There is a secret psychology to money. Most people don't know about it. That's why most people never become financially successful. A lack of money is not the problem; it is merely a symptom of what's going on inside you."

An easy and beautiful way to get an idea of your perception of money is: today, simply look at your bank account—your savings, your investments, your monthly cash flow, and if you're living in the style you desire. By doing this exercise, it's a quick "look" into your consciousness on money. This exercise is not to make you sad or frustrated. Rather, it is to help you identify your relationship to money and, if you choose, create new neural pathways in the brain that reflect what you do want financially.

Looking through an Old Money Lens

Have you ever felt that the amount of money you have is just never enough? Many people feel that way, and this is a great reminder that a "not enough" belief is lurking in your subconscious. I believe how you show up in one part of your life is usually how you show up in other parts of your life.

A person I have known for five years never has enough money. She is always talking about winning the lottery and "if I were rich, I would…." In the five years I've known her, she continues to ask for loans from people and never pays them back, even though she swears that she will. I find her to be a perfect example of having subconscious beliefs around money that keep her poor and frustrated in life, in general. Every frustration centers around not having enough money. There's no reason to judge her, although I find her to be a perfect example of money being an inner game.

I grew up with immigrant parents who came to this country with no money, unable to speak or understand the language, and knowing they had to make a living for their family. We rarely took vacations, went out to dinner, or were lucky enough to have my parents show up at my different awards ceremonies or dance, violin, or piano recitals. I interpreted making money with sacrificing special moments in your child's life. I also learned that you have to work hard to make money and the importance of saving, no matter what!

I made sure that one of my values when I had children was to make the time to be at their sports games, language contests, and anything else they had going on. I also shared with them that I would be happy to be their adult chaperone on school field trips, if they let me know in advance. I absolutely loved being with my children during all these occasions. As a result, we are a very close family and will fly cross country for each other's big events.

However, the immigrant's work ethic had me work extra hard with a lot of hours. Once I realized that my work schedule was based on "hard," I had to do a reality check, and what I found is that, in order to be successful and financially free, you don't have to work all the time—that was an old and outdated belief I had. It's about being focused when working, with healthy time off to refresh! As a result, my work schedule is Monday through Friday; evenings off and weekends off, unless I'm speaking at an event. This schedule has allowed me to exercise and stay fit, receive many Divinely Gifted Downloads that would have taken days to figure out or problem-solve, and it keeps me refreshed and looking forward to each new day.

What Are You Tolerating with Money?

Is there a family code that says: You can't make more than your parents did?

- If I become rich, I would have to sacrifice my health and my family.
- I don't feel I deserve to be wealthy.
- I feel guilty if I make "too much" money.
- I think being humble is being poor.
- Money doesn't grow on trees.

Letting Go with Gratitude

Here's the good news: once you identify your limiting money beliefs, you have the choice to make changes to a higher vibration and positive belief around money. And, if you choose to make changes, then I invite you to let go of the old money consciousness with gratitude. The beauty is to allow yourself without judgment or criticism, to 1) Identify your money situation; 2) Recognize the belief that drives it; 3) Replace it with an "I can do this" belief and attitude; 4) Create a positive financial statement; 5) Visualize the financial life you desire and what you want as vividly as you can and; 6) Get into the feelings of enthusiasm and gratitude for your new and empowered financial life. It's not magic, although it will feel like it, once you focus and commit to this process. Rather than magic, it's really about brain science! Remember, the brain gets its signals and meaning from us, and our subconscious doesn't know what is real or not. So, by continuing these new repetitive thoughts, visualizations, and feelings, you are directly communicating to the part of the brain that listens and listens very well!!

Looking through a New Money Lens

Here are a few suggestions for a supportive financial environment that will help you look through a new lens:

Ask for what you're worth.
Build the confidence in your value.
Stand firm with money negotiations.

Identify a specific amount you will save every week or every paycheck.

Pay off credit card amounts in full each month. If you can't do that, then pay cash or don't make the purchase!!

Pay cash for things for a while, so you can actually SEE how much money $100 really is!

As you save, so you invest, even at a low CD account level or purchase one stock unit...keep your money working for you, 24/7! Find ways to create passive income (this is where your financial adviser comes in handy...you can ask them about this). However, remember that it starts with you and your internal money consciousness.

Generation Why Not?®
Breakthrough Bonus Download #7
DeClutter Check List and Exercises for all three environments
Bonus download here: www.ruthklein.com/why-not-bonuses

Meditation on Clearing Up
Listen to it here: www.ruthklein.com/why-not-bonuses

Song that captures the essence of the chapter:
"Stronger (What Doesn't Kill You)" by Kelly Clarkson

BUSINESS CULTURES WITH PREDOMINANTLY MILLENNIALS, GENERATION X, AND BABY BOOMERS

*"I've learned that people will forget what you said,
people will forget what you did, but people will
never forget how you made them feel."*
Maya Angelou

Conventional wisdom, as incorrect as I have found it to be, says that Millennials are lazy and self-entitled, and expect to be treated well on their first entry-level jobs. Generation X, or the Silent Generation, states that they are more serious in how they see the world, and Baby Boomers are feeling left out and harassed by younger managers who they feel don't understand them and are entitled because of their age.

What I have found to be true through my experience working in business and corporate cultures, giving trainings and workshops, as well as doing executive leadership coaching for the last decade, is that "conventional wisdom" puts an ego judgment on these different groups, without looking at all these people as humans experiencing the same self-limiting beliefs, misidentifications, and misinterpretations from an earlier time period. No matter what the age, the new disruptive shift in the workforce needs to be Attitude…not Age. The values, perceptions, innovative ideas of Generation Why Not?® finally give businesses and corporations new and innovative strategies in solving some of the most complex business, social, and financial problems, working together as a unit, embracing each other's strengths.

It's time to open up the conversation between the "cultural chaos" happening today in business between Millennials, Generation X, and Baby Boomers. We'll look at what is at the core to keep the entrepreneur, employees, and business in alignment for productivity, respectful communication, and intrinsic motivation to be at their jobs. This is becoming more and more essential to integrate into the hallways of business of any size. As we have discussed throughout this book, the Quantum Universe is governed by Intention. And, as a result, your observation and focus become very important.

So how do we integrate Generation Why Not?® using Quantum Synchronicity®: The Method in our businesses and corporations around the world? Before I go into explaining my research and experience, I'd like to talk a little about my findings while doing consulting, executive coaching, and communications training for enterprises ranging from Fortune 500 companies to smaller-sized businesses. I believe these findings are the key elements of transforming business cultures.

As a communications consultant and trainer for a Fortune 500 company, I focused on behavior, personality, and communication skills, no matter the position or the age of the worker. The trainings were so successful that I was asked to come on staff with the company, but I turned it down because I wanted to keep and nurture my own consulting business.

What did we do that opened up the communication between the different age groups?

- We focused on the mission of the company and how the mission of the department projects integrated with that—every company that keeps their mission, as a high-priority Intention gives important follow-up and company culture signals to all the employees.
- We identified, as a group, the top five values that were important to the teams—when values as foundational benchmarks are identified as a group, there is a high level of "buy-in" with everyone present to preserve the integrity of their decisions.
- Whenever a "bone of contention" was expressed, the team went back to their collaborative values and figured out a way to dissolve the issue, literally! The team felt safe to express what wasn't working and knew they would be heard and that, by dissolving the issue, the team became more connected and trustworthy.

- The entire team went through Heart-Centered
  Communication training—how to listen
  without judgment.

As a brand strategist for an upcoming INC 500 company—helping them identify their brand strategy, name the products, and document the uniqueness for each product, and then brainstorming with the executive team—once again I focused on listening, perception-checking to make sure I heard what the person was saying, and watching body language, as 80 percent of our communication is most revealing in body language. Once again, the attitude, not the age, was where I focused. Again, we were so successful working as a team that it only took six months from the day the company called me in to work on their brand for the products to reach retail shelves. It was a team effort! Generation Why Notter Trisha Weldon, CEO, Product Placement Inc., my colleague who recommended me to the company, said, "Because of Ruth's ability to move through this process very quickly while still staying focused on the overall vision, we were able to launch the brand into national retail within six months from our start date, which is literally unheard of."

Why were we able to create the product brand, names, and messaging, and get the products into stores within six months?

- Engaged in collaborative brainstorming, where all recommendations were listened to and honored, even though we may not have used them in the final process.
- Had a representation of all age groups present to balance different outlooks and cultural perceptions.

- Did market analysis to see what was selling and what wasn't selling…and why for each.
- Connected to random potential customers with only three questions.
- Made this a high-priority Intention.
- Took the group through the Quantum Synchronicity®: The Method for valuable insights for brand messaging.

As a brand and marketing consultant, I worked with a big land development company in California. They were developing a large area that, for the previous fifteen years, had faced challenges so serious that the previous companies had gone into bankruptcy. However, this land company knew it had to develop a strong team. They hired me to do their branding and marketing. From the outset, I knew that residents of the entire community would need to feel like they were part of the team as well. In so doing, I took pictures of local people doing normal things in the course of the day and advertised them on billboards in the area. The land developers sold all their properties to builders two years earlier than expected.

What did we do to get those results?

- Maximized community involvement and engagement of family values, lifestyle, and geo-identified outdoor experiences for the area.
- Randomly polled people on the street in nearby communities about what inspired them to move to that area of town.

- Met and spoke with potential builders and realtors.
- Created an "I want to live here" energy.

So what was the common thread among all these different corporate projects? And how did the different ages of the executive team and employees make a difference? As Brian Tracy, motivational speaker and self-development author, says, "Life is like a combination lock; your job is to find the right numbers, in the right order, so you can have anything you want."

So what are the "right numbers" for that combination lock?

Talk about the similarities of each demographic group

There seems to be confusion between the three different age groups and how they can work more harmoniously with each other in business. This seems to be especially evident between the Baby Boomers and the Millennials.

In my consulting and coaching, I hear of this "generation divide," and how it's affecting the harmony of the department, resulting in communication friction, demotivation, turnover, and lack of potential productivity in the aftermath.

I have found that all three age groups can easily command the attention, respect, and potential of one another when certain best practices are put into place. However, before I go into the best practices that have worked, I'd like to focus on some similarities and differences of each group. Here are the birth years of the Baby Boomers, Generation X-ers, and Millennials. Yes, these are "labels," but I invite you to "see" issues of people in all ages, even though these demographics are being used here.

Notice that the Millennials have two distinct age groups with quite different life cycles and needs. This is where some of the "bad rap" placed on Millennials is shaped.

Baby Boomers (1946–1964); Generation X (1965–1980); Millennials (1977–1994 and 1981–2000—two different groups within one larger group).

I'd like to share the similarities and differences for each in four areas: core values, work ethic, variations in the workplace, and preferred communication style.

Core Values

Baby Boomers: Ambitious, challenge authority, competent, competitive, idealism, live to work and now looking for work/life balance, rebellious against convention, strong "traditional" work ethic, independent, me-attitude in work and life, optimistic, work ethic and "face time" are important, value personal growth, continuing education, making a contribution

Generation X-ers: Antiestablishment, see gap with Baby Boomers, confident, competent, irritated, flexible, focused on results, self-starters, strong sense of entitlement from parents, rather unimpressed with authority, looking for work/life balance and work to live, independent, self-absorbed, look for meaningful work.

Millennials: Ambitious, love working in teams, the best-educated group so far, very independent, focus is on family, global citizens, close to parents, creative, me-first attitude in work and life, optimistic, self-absorbed, high level of general anxiety, sense of entitlement, crave mentorship on the job, balance with work/life/community, value personal growth, look for meaningful work and where they can move forward, OK with "older" leadership, looking to leadership/mentors/ managers to further their work skills and continuing education, want to make a contribution.

Work Ethic

Baby Boomers: Driven with fifty- to sixty-hour work weeks, focused on relationships and results, work as a career or work to retire, like achieving results with teams. However, many Boomers today are looking for work/life balance, as they sacrificed fun for work.

Generation X-ers: Balance and work smarter with more productivity over more hours, appreciate and crave structure and direction, skeptical of authority and leadership, focused on the results of tasks, looking for innovation, view work as a contract/job.

Millennials: Very entrepreneurial and always looking for the next task to do, focused globally and being part of a network, good workers although ready to leave punctually when the workday ends, motivated by learning and self-development in the workplace, very interested in flex-time and job sharing, work ethic suggested this group will request sabbaticals more often, looking for innovation, want continuous feedback, work is fulfillment-oriented, like working in teams, they feel their time at a company is limited.

Variations in the Workplace

Baby Boomers: Expect everyone to be workaholics and put in their "time," very patient and comfortable with delayed gratification, mission oriented, don't take criticism well, like clear goals and expectations.

Generation X-ers: Impatient, skeptical of the optimism of their "bookend" workers (Boomers and Millennials), people skills could be improved, task-oriented, do not like to be lectured to, require clear goals and expectations, many are irritated and don't know why.

Millennials: Impatient, people skills—particularly with difficult people—can be improved, task-oriented, do not like to be lectured to, especially by "older" people or leadership, high expectations at work, need clear goals and expectations and welcome mentoring help on these.

Preferred Communication Style

Baby Boomers: Do well with flexibility, attention and freedom, appreciate work/life balance—particularly if they're part of the Boomer "sandwich" age, when they're taking care of children/grandchildren and aging parents, focus on the company's mission, like feedback.

Generation X-ers: Do well with flexibility, attention, and freedom; appreciate any help with their work/life balance; listen in short sound bites; want feedback; time off is a big benefit; like variety; expect follow-through of managers; very much into experiences.

Millennials: Do well with flexibility, lavish attention, and supportive and mentored work environment; appreciate any help or feedback on keeping their work/life balance; love a participative environment; listen in short sound bites; need feedback often; time off is a big benefit; would love a customized work plan; like variety; expect follow-through of managers; very much into experiences.

Best Practices in Creating a Motivating, Harmonious, and Productive Work Environment

Let's look at ways to incorporate the "variations" and "similarities" into a workable plan to be used and implemented in business. How does management prepare for this new Paradigm Shift in workers' values, work ethic, and communication styles?

Here are some best practices that help facilitate companies to move past the variations and focus on the similarities. And the secret ingredient is to understand behavioral psychology of people, no matter their age. There are certain things that most people respond well to. Let's focus on those here. Behavioral psychology looks at the connection between what we're thinking, our minds, and how it affects how we act, our behavior. It tries to understand why people behave the way they do and find patterns to help in understanding them.

So let's take a step back and look at what most people respond positively to. The idea, as I have experienced, is to create opportunities for everyone in the company to feel motivated by their positions and the communications within their departments. If we look at the basic foundation of the psychology of learning, we find that, very simplistically, there are three types of learning conditioning: classical conditioning, which included Pavlov's renowned experiment that the smell of food was the stimulus associated with the ringing of the bell; operant conditioning, where the probability of a response will increase with reinforcement and diminish with punishment; and observational learning, which happens through observation or imitation, or imprinting. As Austrian zoologist Konrad Lorenz showed: "Incubator-hatched geese were imprinted with the first moving stimulus they saw within thirteen to sixteen hours after being hatched."

So what do these three types of learning conditioning have to do with business culture and intergenerational communications?

I have seen and trained in all three learning conditioning modalities to reach and impact the organization, no matter their age.

For example, how many times do you get a visceral feeling when a boss or manager drops by, or the visceral feeling you may receive with feedback from leadership? The neutral stimulus is your boss, and he/she is associated with a positive feeling or a fearful feeling.

Operant learning is based on positive reinforcement for the behavior you want to see more of and negative reinforcement, which is considered to be punishment for the worker.

Observational learning is how employees learn the internal culture of a company by observing and doing similar kinds of things, imitating what they see and hear in order to be part of the whole.

Within these learning conditioning modalities lie three specific learning styles: visual (what you see), auditory (through hearing), and kinesthetic (physical touch and doing experientially). The manager, trainer, parent, or community leader who integrates all three types of learning will touch the learning centers of the people they're working and communicating with.

And, finally, there's a third layer to learning. Some people prefer to work alone (solitary), and others prefer to work in groups (social).

Looking across all the different demographic groups, one can now start to make sense of the learning modalities, because each person, at any age, consists of more than the birth dates and cultural circumstances of that era. Rather, to empower your employees, family members, and community leaders is to help them see that the external circumstances do not define them. Rather, it is the *meaning* we give external circumstances that defines us.

There are two quotes by Viktor Emil Frankl, an Austrian psychologist as well as a Holocaust survivor, that represent this new disruptive perception beautifully:

> *"When we are no longer able to change a situation,*
> *we are challenged to change ourselves."*

> *"Everything can be taken from a man but one thing: the*
> *last of the human freedoms—to choose one's attitude in*
> *any given set of circumstances, to choose one's own way."*

Seven Effective Management Leadership Skills

Management is a very important role model in any organization, no matter how small or large. And the most effective managers I've worked with and trained are those who are also effective leaders. Here are seven effective management leadership skills that promote harmonious internal communication, employee motivation, productivity, talent, and creativity in business.

1. Giving effective feedback in a way that motivates rather than demotivates the worker. Some people require more continuous feedback than others. This is not really an age thing; it is more of a personality thing. Usually, people who are highly competent and are perfectionists require more feedback and guidance. Inspire and motivate your employees to execute the company's vision and positively reinforce them often.

2. Showing respect to the other person by allowing them to speak, maintaining eye contact with them when speaking, listening while not judging, following up on what you said you would do for the person or the department, and allowing access to you, while focusing on employee's strengths.

3. Practicing heart-centered listening, which requires you to allow the other person to speak without trying to figure out what to say next or be defensive in your response. It also has you open up to listening without judging what they're saying. Think of listening with neutral ears and curiosity.

4. Perception-checking that summarizes what the person has said to make sure you understand what they mean. If that is not what they are trying to say, they will say something like, "Well, not exactly," or "No, what I was trying to say is…," or "Yes, that is correct." When someone feels heard, they feel that they count, that they matter. All age groups want to feel seen, feel valuable, and feel that they and the work they do matter.

5. Modeling 100 percent Personal Responsibility for your thoughts, actions, and communication with your team and within your department. There's no blaming, shaming, or guilt trips given…ever! Your team learns (via modeling and imprinting) to do the same as a result, always supporting and promoting your team (positive reinforcement). This is also where the manager leads in teaching systems, processes, and making sure everyone understands them and has experienced them (kinesthetic).

6. Modeling enjoyment of your role and what you're doing, staying positive and looking at all issues or mistakes as learning, and how being open to new options of a different way of solving the issue is the best path to follow. And offering ongoing self-development and skills development. Embracing and staying alert to new research and technology in your area, as well as in other areas of business. It comes down to leading with curiosity, not judgment.

7. Engaging with employees to innovate and create participatory and fun team projects for those who prefer social

interaction in the work environment, as well as innovative and fun projects for the person who prefers to work alone. Encourage them to think outside the box, to take inspired action when Intuition strikes.

Simply stated, effective management leadership is not age-driven but rather, is driven by communicating, listening, and training.

POWERFUL IMPLICATIONS IN BUSINESS, FAMILIES, AND COMMUNITIES

"It is by going down into the abyss that we recover the treasures of life. Where you stumble, there lies your treasure."
Joseph Campbell

So how can we impart this new perceptual shift in business, families, and community? And how do we get the conversation going in a big way that truly touches the hearts of millions of people? Here are a few powerful implications of how the Generation Why Not?® internal values, mindset, and code of communication exist with all its stakeholders, upending the old structure of only holding shareholders' interests in business as important.

Generation Why Not?® Perceptual
Lens in Business

Business Roundtable—Large Corporations:

An editorial in the San Francisco Chronicle entitled "Redefining corporate value" examined how the Business Roundtable, made up of several hundred leaders of America's biggest companies, was redefining what it means to be a successful corporation moving forward. Their definition of "the purpose of a corporation" is changing. The old definition was "that shareholders' interests should exceed all other concerns." They have now changed it to say: "We share a fundamental commitment to all our stakeholders," including customers, employees, suppliers, communities, and shareholders. "Americans deserve an economy that allows each person to succeed through hard work and creativity and to live a life of meaning and dignity," reads the statement of the organization chaired by JPMorgan Chase CEO Jamie Dimon.

B Corporations:

A certified B corporation is defined as "businesses that meet the highest standards of verified social and environmental performance, public transparency, and legal accountability to balance profit and purpose. There is a global movement of people that see their businesses, large and small, as a force for good, longevity, sustainability and, as they balance profits and the greater good of all stakeholders, called B Lab, which includes those companies that are certified B corporations and those that have integrated the values and sustainability for their businesses, including non-profits." The B Lab says, "B Lab is a non-profit organization for non-profits who promote mission-aligned legal structures, like the benefit corporation, that join the interests of business with those of society. These new corporate forms give entrepreneurs the freedom to define success beyond profit for their businesses and protect their mission through changes in ownership and leadership. B Lab collaborates with businesses, the capital markets, and policymakers to drive adoption of these structures around the world."

For-profit one-for-one social mission:

CommonBond's website says: *"A force for good…Every time we fund a loan, we cover the cost of a child's education through our Social Promise. Our partnership with Pencils of Promise has provided schools, teachers, and technology to thousands of students in the developing world."*

David Klein, co-founder and CEO of CommonBond, says they have been able to donate over $1 million to Pencils of Promise to date.

Generation Why Not?® Perceptual Lens in Families

Less codependency, learn to be responsible for their thoughts; more harmony and respectful communication.

Conscious Loving—Conscious loving in families focuses on seeing the loving essence of each person in the family, no matter what. It is a process of staying present and connected to your Higher Self first, and then connecting to each person in the family from this internal place. Using Quantum Synchronicity®: The Method is the perfect blueprint for this type of Big Love. I have found through experience, research, and with clients, that the Big Love must first start with yourself. That means, you love and accept who you are, with all your imperfections, and are able to withhold from any self-deprecation, shaming, feeling guilty, or blaming yourself or others, in terms of where your life is today.

Doctors Gay and Kathlyn Hendricks have written several books and offer seminars on conscious loving for decades. You may want to check out some of their books.

Conscious Parenting—A friend of mind, Sonny, grew up in a family with alcoholic parents and ended up using alcohol to, as she says, "numb" her feelings. Sonny always felt irritable and angry, even though she didn't know why. She decided to change and become sober, even though her husband and her social life friends still drank. Six months into her sobriety, her husband, without being mocked or asked by her, said he wanted to feel the same emotional high he saw his wife experience within the family toward him and their young children. She became aware of and present to her "empty feelings," and journals all of them for insight and the ability to let them go. She no longer uses alcohol when trying to deal with stress or challenges and made a pivotal decision to be a different type of parent than what she grew up with, to be conscious and not "sleepwalk" through life while raising her children.

Conscious Divorce—Lori, a family attorney in LA, and Jessie, a family attorney in Orange County, have both independently started partnering with Conscious life coaches to help ease the difficult transition of divorce with all family members—spouses as well as the children.

Universal Mom®—This is the new nonprofit that I'm starting up that is extending The Self-Esteem Council of twenty-two years. The Universal Mom's message is: "Helping children and teens uncover their brilliance, talents, and uniqueness through the art of writing."

There's more information at www.UniversalMom.org.

Generation Why Not?® Perceptual Lens in Communities

Strong communities acting as the all-important support systems we know make a positive difference in the lives of the community.

Conscious Inclusion—One of my clients and dear friends, Elaine Hall, founded The Miracle Project. Its website says: "The Miracle Project is a fully inclusive theatre, film, and expressive arts program for children, teens, and adults with autism and all abilities. Using groundbreaking and evidence-based methods developed by our award-winning founder, Elaine Hall, The

Miracle Project focuses on the strengths and abilities inherent in its participants, providing tools to build communication, social skills, job skills, and friendships while developing a unique neuro-diverse community." In fact, one of her Miracle Project students, Coby Bird, is a professional actor now who is autistic and has been on several television shows. He says, "I want to be an actor and make people laugh and cry. I love being able to play characters and tell their stories." I asked Coby what he had to believe to make acting a reality and his reply was, "I had to believe in myself."

Education—"Genius Hour in the classroom is an approach to learning built around student curiosity, self-directed learning, and passion-based work." If this sounds like something Google does in the workplace, then you're correct! How would using what I refer to as the Google Creative Time work in any business or organization? Can you imagine offering 20 percent of your employees' time be working on projects they're passionate about or have a keen interest in? How would that contribute new ideas, creative approaches to problem-solving, or innovative ways for participation, productivity, and profits?

Generation Why Not?® Perceptual Lens in Health

We know more about the brain in the last ten to twelve years than we have in the last fifty. It is a very exciting time to be alive and be part of this new conscious perceptual shift happening all around us, including in health.

Cardiology—Dr. Dean Ornish, MD, cardiologist and author, has promoted the idea that you can reverse heart disease for over twenty years, even though his cohorts originally didn't acknowledge this to be true when he first started. He believes that a person with heart disease can reverse it through exercise, meditation, diet, and talk discussions. I remember giving Dr. Dean Ornish's book, *You Can Reverse Heart Disease,* to my dad over twenty years ago when my dad had his first heart attack. Somehow, it was easier for my dad to believe it was better to take pills for his heart than try to reverse the disease.

Dr. Bruce Lipton—He has proven that genes do not determine our destiny and that our thoughts are more powerful than our genes in health and healing.

Many powerful implications arise out of creating a harmonious environment in business, families, and communities. And much has been happening to make the idea of living a life that's more fulfilling, healthy, and joy filled for yourself and others you communicate with. I have often said it only takes one person to get this started. It has to start somewhere, and my question to you is: *Why not* you?

Here's the deal: So many people are just existing and feeling trapped in their lives with no way open for future happiness. And much of our happiness is related to how we see the world... the lens from which we interpret everything we observe, experience, and live. I find it extraordinary that there exists a conscious system, Quantum Synchronicity®: The Method, that helps you explore who you are, your passions, what makes you tick, what holds you back, and where your upset is coming from, and offers a huge window of opportunity to find all your experiences a blessing and that you, and only you, can take yourself out of being a victim—who things happen to—and become someone who has the control to create the type of life, business, family, community, and health that you envision but may not be a reality at this time.

Now that we know that the future is created right now—with your Intentions, Thoughts, Beliefs, Decisions, and Actions—you have a blueprint to experiment with. I often like to think of myself as a social scientist when I start creating a new dream and have the Intention for its manifestation. I'll share a few things I intended and manifested:

I always wanted to live near the ocean where I could see the white waters and hear the waves crash. I live in a condo overlooking the ocean with all those Intentions.

I always wanted to have a close family unit. Even though I divorced several years ago, my "ex" and I are friends, and my children and I have a very close, loving, and respectful relationship.

I always saw myself as a professional woman, and I started my professional consulting, training, and coaching business over twenty-five years ago.

I wanted a house with a garden, and last December, I purchased one.

I always kept my eye on taking whatever extra cash flow came in and investing it in real estate. My passive income from the real estate allows me to live in financial freedom.

I wanted to do something impactful with children. I started a non-profit organization called, The Self-Esteem Council, with three other beautiful women and it positively impacted high school students for twenty-two years!

"Social Scientist" Past Experiment

I used the Quantum Synchronicity® blueprint before I coined the term, over twenty-four years ago. I wanted to create an enrichment program for children that would increase their self-esteem. In the work that I do, the most basic element of someone being successful is how they perceive themselves. A high level of self-esteem helps children weather negative dips, and a child with low self-esteem may easily get caught up in the negative dips.

Here is how I used the Social Scientist experiment:

Intention: My Intention is to create an enrichment program for high school students that is positive and loving, and embraces who they are as individuals, with the sole purpose of building their self-esteem to be in a stronger position to take on life's journey.

Thought: I need help in putting this together and brainstorming different ways to do this in a safe environment.

I'll ask four of my friends to be on the nonprofit Self-Esteem Council board, and we will create this together.

Belief: Teaching children about self-esteem at a school with the school behind us, we can ask the school if we can take thirty minutes of one class and their lunchtime for the class.

Decision: We decided to create a "Lunch & Learn" program and that the school counselors will choose the students who are falling between the cracks in the classroom and perhaps socially. We decided to work with two groups during the school year for five months each, doubling up one month. We also decided to focus on sophomore girls first, then open it up to junior and senior girls and boys.

Action: We started the Lunch & Learn program.

Momentum: We started in one high school, then we found more mentors to volunteer, and we had up to forty-five mentors volunteering in seven high schools. I urged the board to grow into other cities but was voted down each time I suggested it.

Once a year, we had a community fundraising lunch at my home, where we would raise enough money for the following year for the students.

This program continued for twenty-two years with the same board for that entire time!

Environment: We wanted each Lunch & Learn class to be inviting, pretty, and nutritious. There were four to five mentors per class, and one of the mentors would make the food, one would bring the drinks, one would take the nice dishes and silverware home (we bought the silverware and dishes at the dollar store or a thrift store), one mentor would bring her holiday decorations from home for the table, and one mentor would lead the discussion. We used our own pretty tablecloths as well. Everything we did, including how to set the lunch table, where the silverware is placed, the proper etiquette with napkins, and how to chew food, emphasized learning to listen when others spoke.

The environment was fun, joyful, and loving, and, with everything we did, we knew we were imprinting new ways for these children to see the world.

Results: The Self-Esteem Council program was incredibly successful. Here are a few of the results of being with these students for slightly less than ten hours!!! It doesn't take long to make a big impact. What it does take, however, is a pure and clear Intention, Positive Thoughts, a Strong and Embracing Belief about finding the goodness and powers of others, the Courage and Commitment of the decision to move forward, Inspired Action that is positive and whose high vibrational energy is felt by others, Positive Reinforcement for the behavior you seek that only keeps the positive flow of behavior alive, and the Environment where you know that all that you do, how you act, how you see the world, will translate into new learning through imprinting, reinforcement, and observation. It's a win, win, win, win for everyone. Win for us as mentors, win for the students, win for the communities, and win for the schools.

This is what "for the greater good of all" refers to! I like to put this phrase at the end of any of my Intentions. It reminds me to create a win-win-win-win scenario. This is where, I believe, we can and do make the biggest impact in our business, our families, and our communities.

My Wish and Intention for You:
To experience a deepening awareness of the Divine
Loving Essence within you and others;
To "see" your challenges as your blessings;
To feel the fear and then let it go as it dissolves into love
to become one of your greatest sources of strength;
To act courageously and take inspired action;
To be open to the possibility of "Why Not?";
To communicate with curiosity, rather than judgment;
To embrace a "can do" attitude for yourself and others;
To encourage a new perceptual shift welcoming all peo-
ple of all types to live in beauty and freedom;
To spread your financial, emotional, and intel-
lectual prosperity for the good of all;
And…for your new story to BE the liv-
ing Miracle you are and desire.
May you live your life in the Miracle Field
with joy, courage, and love!
Why Not?

Generation Why Not?® Sources
B Corporations and B Lab, www.BCorporations.net
Rasiel, Ethan, *The McKinsey Way*, New
York: McGraw-Hill, 1999
West Midland Family Center, www.wmfc.org,
Generational Similarities and Differences Chart

ACKNOWLEDGMENTS

I've been on an incredible journey writing this book and through it all, I can say that I have learned things about myself, my surroundings, and writing this book truly felt like giving birth. Along the way I was supported by so many kindred Spirits! I am truly grateful to all of the inspirational and heart-centered Generation Why Not?® interviewees who shared their stories and their hearts with me for the purpose of getting this message out into the world, by sharing their experiences.

My amazing Generation Why Not?® clients who have taught me so much about integrity, dignity, passion, and purpose of the human spirit. Thank you, my precious friends.

To my dear friends, Erin Leatherman, Zach Tanenbaum, Hang Boge, Theresa Mawson, Sandy Morton, Tanya Memme, Ruth Garcia, Cat Lambertini, Lorri Herman, Elaine Hall, Renee Piane, Karmen Reed, Marc Clark, Jethro Singer, Papa Soob and so many other beautiful hearts who put up with my writing schedule, even though we didn't spend much time together.

My incredible literary agent, Dana Newman, who believed in my project from the start and introduced me to one of my favorite coffee places, Milo & Olive; my publicist extraordinaire, Dennis Welsh, who made sure my book got into the right hands and is helping spread the Generation Why Not?® movement; to Alan Reed, general manager of The Landing at Morro Bay Motel, my secret writing haven. Alan and his team provided me with anything I needed to make my experience over-the-top wonderful! Ed Rampell, you helped make my words dance. Thank you to the Post Hill Press team and especially Maddie Sturgeon, who kindly extended my manuscript deadline three times without putting any pressure on me…that is a feat!

To my beautiful and loving children—Naomi, David, Erica, Daniel, Jessica, and all seven "little ones" who were supportive of my "absence" while writing the book. I can't even begin to tell you how much I love, appreciate, and respect all of you!!!

And, I dedicate this book to my dear and sweet friend, Judy Fairchild, who was an Angel in this lifetime and has since gone to meet other Angels in Heaven. You were and continue to be one of my biggest champions of love, grace, kindness, and support. I often hear your words, "Ruthie, be the best you can be and remember to dance."

Thank you all for making my life that much richer, fuller, and more meaningful!!